The Power of Place: Master

Advanced Aspect-Based Astrocartography

Gianna Succi

AstroGiagraphy

The Power of Place: Master

Timing and Transit Strategies in Astrocartography

Copyright © 2025 by Gianna Succi

All rights reserved. No part of this book may be reproduced, stored in a retrieval system, or transmitted in any form or by any means—electronic, mechanical, photocopying, recording, or otherwise—without prior written permission from the author, except for brief quotations in critical reviews or articles.

First Edition

ISBN: 979-8-9942531-1-3

Published by AstroGiagraphy

Book 3 of The Power of Place trilogy

Also in this series:

The Power of Place: Discover — Foundation Guide to Reading Your Astrocartography Map

The Power of Place: Navigate — Timing and Transit Strategies in Astrocartography

Disclaimer

The information in this book is for educational and entertainment purposes only. Astrocartography is a tool for self-discovery and should not replace professional advice regarding major life decisions, legal matters, financial planning, medical concerns, or mental health support.

Contact

Website: AstroGiagraphy.com

Printed in the United States of America

Acknowledgements

To the places I've been, To where I am, And where I will be going.

To all the people I have met along the way— Those who still walk beside me, Those who no longer do, And those who are yet to come.

I am grateful and I thank you

Foreword

On December 19, 2025, I planted the seed of *The Power of Place* by publishing the first book of the series: *Discover* under a New Moon in Sagittarius conjunct my natal Vertex. That was about beginning. About stepping forward to teach. About courage.

Today, I deliberately release the final book of this series, *Master*, under the Wolf Supermoon in Cancer.

This Full Moon falls at 18 degrees Cancer in my twelfth house—the house of endings and spiritual release—conjunct Jupiter at 21 degrees. A supermoon occurs when the Moon is closest to Earth, appearing larger and brighter than usual. This is the last of four consecutive supermoons and won't appear again until November. Jupiter in Cancer is exalted, operating at peak benevolence, blessing this completion.

The supermoon trines my natal Pluto at 14 degrees Scorpio in my fourth house—the heart of my work around place, home, and transformation. The Sun in Capricorn sextiles my Pluto, creating opportunity for this teaching to endure. Cancer asks *where is home?* Capricorn answers *what you've built will last.*

January 3rd is also when Earth reaches perihelion—our closest point to the Sun. A supermoon coinciding with perihelion is rare, happening once every nineteen years. Earth, Moon, and Sun are at their closest together, an alignment that won't occur again until 2045.

This isn't random timing. It's partnership with cosmic rhythm.

Throughout this series, you've learned to read your astrocartography map, understand planetary energies across geography, master timing alongside placement, and apply advanced techniques with confidence. What began as one seed under a New Moon reaches fullness under a Supermoon—a complete teaching, a foundation others can build upon.

I'm releasing this not because the work is perfect, but because it's complete. Because the Full Moon says the cycle is whole. Because Jupiter blesses this completion. Because this rare alignment marks sacred time.

We plant seeds on new moons. We harvest on full moons.

The Power of Place ends here, under this Wolf Supermoon conjunct Jupiter, as I return home from this journey.

Welcome home.

Contents

Introduction	IX
1. The Hidden Layer: How Natal Aspects Transform Your Lines	1
2. Mapping Your Unique Aspect Web	12
3. When Transits Meet Your Aspect Web	19
4. Harmonious Aspects: Trines and Sextiles in Your Web	30
5. Challenging Aspects: Squares and Oppositions in Your Web	49
6. Mixed Aspect Patterns: When Harmonious and Challenging Aspects Combine	70
7. Special Points at Professional Depth	75
8. Strategic Decision-Making: Integrating Aspects, Transits, and Timing	104
9. Aspects to Special Points: The Hidden Modifiers	114
10. T-Squares: Navigating Maximum Pressure Points	137
11. Grand Trines: The Gift and the Trap of Ease	147
12. Stelliums: Concentrated Power and Strategic Direction	157
13. Transit Timing: When to Activate Which Lines	168

14.	Real-World Case Studies: Theory Meets Practice	181
15.	Creating Your Personal Astrocartography Strategy	187
Conclusion		193
Glossary		200
Index		208

Introduction

You've learned to read your astrocartography map. You know your Sun line brings confidence, your Moon line feels like home, and your Venus line attracts love and beauty. You've learned strategic timing: when to travel during supportive transits and when to avoid challenging ones. You've chosen destinations based on planetary meanings and optimal timing windows. You've done everything the books told you to do. And still, something doesn't quite fit.

Your friend Sarah raved about her Venus line in Paris, describing it as the most magical romantic experience of her entire life. She met her future husband within a month of arriving, found a charming apartment through an impossible series of fortunate coincidences, and spent two years feeling like she was living in a fairy tale. You heard her stories and thought, 'Yes. That's exactly what I want.'

So you planned carefully. You traveled to Barcelona on your Venus line during a Jupiter transit, supposedly the most fortunate timing possible. Venus for love and beauty, Jupiter for expansion and luck. The astrocartography books and the transit books all said this should be incredible. You arrived full of hope and excitement.

Instead, you found yourself in an intense, obsessive relationship that consumed you. Beautiful, yes. Passionate, absolutely. But also volatile, jealous, and ultimately destructive. You were simultaneously drawn in and pushed away, experiencing extremes of connection and separation. It didn't feel like Sarah's fairy tale. It felt like a psychological thriller. You started wondering what you'd done wrong, or whether astrocartography even works, or if you were somehow broken or cursed.

Here's what nobody told you: Sarah's natal Venus forms a close trine to Jupiter, a harmonious, flowing aspect that makes Venusian experiences naturally fortunate and expansive. Your natal Venus squares Pluto, an intense, transformative aspect that makes Venusian experiences deep, powerful, and psychologically complex. You both traveled to your Venus lines. You both activated Venus energy. But you activated completely different Venus experiences because you have completely different Venus patterns built into your natal charts.

Or consider another scenario. Every astrocartography book warns you to avoid Saturn lines. They say Saturn is restrictive, challenging, heavy: a place of hard lessons and necessary but difficult growth. Your friend Michael ignored this advice and moved to Denver on his Saturn IC line anyway. He described it as one of the most rewarding experiences of his life. Yes, he worked harder than ever, but he also built something lasting, developed genuine maturity, and felt deeply rooted and secure for the first time. He couldn't understand why the books made Saturn sound so terrible.

What Michael didn't know, and what the books didn't explain, is that his natal Saturn forms a grand trine with his Sun and Moon in earth signs. Saturn and the luminaries work together harmoniously in his chart, creating natural discipline, practical wisdom, and grounded achievement. His Saturn line didn't feel crushing because his natal Saturn isn't crushing. It's supportive, strengthening, and foundational. The line amplified his natal pattern, which happened to be workable and even empowering.

Meanwhile, your other friend Rachel moved to the same city, Denver, also on her Saturn IC line. She described it as one of the most difficult periods of her life: isolated, depressed, struggling with every aspect of daily existence. Same city. Same planetary line. Completely different experience. Why? Because Rachel's natal Saturn squares her Sun and opposes her Moon. Her natal Saturn creates friction, restriction, and emotional difficulty. Her Saturn line amplified that pattern, making it overwhelmingly present.

This is the hidden variable that most astrocartography practitioners never learn, never teach, and honestly might not even know exists: natal aspects fundamentally transform how every planetary line manifests.

You weren't missing anything from the first two books. You weren't doing anything wrong. You were simply ready for the third level of understanding: the key that unlocks why your lines feel uniquely yours in ways that generic planetary interpretations can never predict.

Welcome to The Power of Place: Master, the final book in the trilogy and the revelation that completes the astrocartography system. While Discover taught you where your lines are and Navigate taught you when to use them, Master teaches you how your natal aspects modify everything, creating experiences that can't be predicted from planetary meanings or transit timing alone.

Your natal aspects are the geometric relationships between planets in your birth chart: the trines, squares, sextiles, oppositions, and conjunctions that link different planetary energies together. These aspects fundamentally alter how each planet expresses itself in every area of your life, including geographically.

Your Venus doesn't exist in isolation. It's woven into a web of connections with other planets. When you travel to your Venus line, you don't just activate Venus. You activate every planet that aspects your

Venus simultaneously. If your Venus trines Jupiter and squares Saturn, those connections come alive too. You're not experiencing generic Venus energy. You're experiencing your specific Venus-Jupiter-Saturn web, which creates an entirely different reality than someone whose Venus trines Neptune and sextiles Mars.

This is the hidden layer. This is why two people on the same planetary line have completely different experiences. It's not random. It's not about one person being more evolved, more lucky, or more spiritually aligned. It's about natal aspects modifying how each line manifests for each unique chart.

I discovered this truth through years of client work and personal experimentation. I kept seeing patterns that didn't make sense based on planetary line meanings alone. Clients would return from travels confused because their experiences didn't match the interpretations. I'd see people thrive on lines that should have been challenging, and struggle on lines that should have been supportive. The standard interpretations were clearly missing something crucial.

The breakthrough came when I started systematically analyzing the natal aspects of planets involved in surprising line experiences. Every single time someone had an unexpected outcome on a planetary line, I found natal aspects that explained the deviation from standard interpretation. The Venus-Pluto square explained intense, obsessive Venus line experiences. The Saturn grand trine explained empowering, strengthening Saturn line experiences. The patterns were consistent, predictable, and remarkably accurate once I knew to look for them.

This discovery transformed my entire practice. Suddenly I could explain experiences that had seemed random or contradictory. I could predict with far greater accuracy how someone would experience a particular line, not just based on the planet involved, but based on their complete natal aspect web. Most importantly, I could help people make genuinely informed decisions about where to go and when, decisions based on their unique cosmic blueprint rather than generic planetary meanings.

Most astrocartography practitioners never reach this level of interpretation. They work with planetary lines in isolation, missing the aspect layer entirely. This keeps their readings accurate only at a general level: correct about broad themes but unable to explain or predict the specific quality of experiences. This book reveals that hidden layer and teaches you how to work with it strategically.

You'll learn exactly which planets activate when you travel to any line. You'll understand how to predict whether a line will feel harmonious or challenging based on your natal aspects. You'll discover how to combine aspect analysis with transit timing for unprecedented precision in location planning. You'll develop the ability to look at your chart and immediately see which lines offer natural advantage, which require conscious work, and which demand extraordinary support systems to navigate safely.

This is mastery-level astrocartography. This is where theory becomes personalized strategy, where generic interpretations transform into precise predictions, where you stop following general advice and start working with your unique cosmic blueprint.

By the end of this book, you'll understand why your lines feel the way they do. You'll know which lines will work best for your unique chart and life circumstances. You'll be able to make location decisions based on complete information rather than partial planetary meanings. You'll look at upcoming transits and know exactly which natal aspects they'll activate in different locations, giving you unprecedented strategic power for travel and relocation planning.

If Discover gave you the map and Navigate gave you the calendar, Master gives you the key to your personal code. Together, the three books create a complete system for conscious, strategic, deeply personalized geographic alignment with your soul's journey.

The cosmos speaks in many languages. Planetary placement is one. Transit timing is another. But natal aspects are the secret dialect: the hidden grammar that transforms standard meanings into your unique story. You're about to become fluent.

Welcome to The Power of Place: Master. Let's unlock your unique map.

Chapter One

The Hidden Layer: How Natal Aspects Transform Your Lines

Two people stand at the same intersection in Prague, both living on their Venus Descendant lines. Sarah meets the love of her life within weeks, falls into an easy, joyful relationship, and describes Prague as the most romantic city she's ever experienced. David meets someone who initially seems perfect but the relationship becomes obsessive, possessive, and ultimately destructive. He leaves Prague heartbroken and confused. Same line. Same city. Completely different experiences.

This isn't random. This isn't about one person being luckier or more spiritually evolved. The difference lies in something most astrocartography practitioners don't discuss: natal aspects. Sarah's natal Venus trines Jupiter and sextiles Neptune, creating a harmonious web of romantic ease and spiritual connection. David's natal Venus squares Pluto and opposes Mars, creating a pattern of intense, transformative, sometimes volatile relationship dynamics. When they both activate their Venus lines, they don't just activate Venus. They activate their entire Venus pattern, every planet that aspects their natal Venus simultaneously springs to life.

This is the hidden layer of astrocartography that transforms interpretation from generic planetary meanings into precise, personalized understanding. This chapter introduces the fundamental principle that will change how you work with your astrocartography map forever.

Why Your Lines Feel Different Than Others

If you've explored astrocartography with friends or in online communities, you've probably noticed something puzzling. Someone raves about their Saturn line, describing it as grounding, strengthening, and powerfully maturing. You visit your Saturn line expecting similar benefits and instead feel restricted, blocked, and depressed. Someone else describes their Jupiter line as overwhelming, scattered, and excessive. You visit your Jupiter line and experience abundant opportunity, lucky breaks, and effortless expansion. What's happening?

Standard astrocartography interpretation treats planetary lines as if they have universal meanings. Venus lines bring love and beauty. Mars lines bring energy and action. Saturn lines bring discipline and structure. These baseline interpretations aren't wrong, but they're incomplete. They describe the planetary archetype in isolation, ignoring the fact that no planet in your birth chart exists in isolation. Every planet is connected to other planets through aspects, and these aspect connections fundamentally alter how that planet's energy expresses.

The Web vs. The Line

Think of your natal chart not as a collection of separate planetary positions but as an interconnected web of relationships. Mars doesn't just represent your drive and assertion. Mars in relationship to Venus (through aspects) describes how desire and aggression interact in your psyche. Mars in relation to Saturn describes how drive and discipline balance or conflict. Mars in relationship to Jupiter describes how action and expansion combine or clash.

When you travel to your Mars line, you don't just activate Mars in isolation. You activate the entire Mars web. Every planet that aspects your natal Mars wakes up geographically. If your Mars trines Jupiter, that trine activates too. If your Mars squares Saturn, that square activates too. The line is just the entry point. The web is what actually manifests in your experience.

This explains why two people on the same planetary line have such different experiences. They're not activating the same planetary energy. They're activating their unique planetary webs, which may be entirely different in structure, harmony, and challenge. Your Mars-Jupiter trine web feels nothing like someone else's Mars-Saturn square web, even though you're both technically on Mars lines.

The Myth of Good and Bad Lines

In astrocartography communities, certain lines develop reputations. Venus and Jupiter lines are celebrated as beneficial, desirable, worth planning trips around. Saturn and Pluto lines are often avoided, feared, or approached with caution. This oversimplification causes unnecessary anxiety and misses tremendous opportunity.

There are no universally good or bad lines. There are only lines that activate your particular aspect of the web in ways that feel harmonious or challenging depending on your natal chart structure. A Saturn line with harmonious aspects to other planets in your chart can be profoundly strengthening, grounding, and maturing. A Venus line with challenging aspects can bring difficult relationships, values conflicts, or painful lessons about pleasure and worth.

The key shift in understanding is moving from judging lines as inherently positive or negative to understanding how your unique aspect pattern modifies that line's expression. Saturn isn't the problem.

Your natal Saturn's relationship to other planets determines whether Saturn line activation feels like masterful discipline or crushing limitation. Venus isn't automatically wonderful. Your natal Venus's relationships determine whether Venus line activation brings joyful romance or painful obsession.

Real Examples: Same Line, Different Webs

Let's examine three people, all living on their Saturn IC lines, to see how natal aspects completely transform the experience of the same planetary line in the same angular position.

Michael: Saturn Trine Sun, Sextile Moon

Michael relocated to Denver, which fell on his Saturn IC line. His natal Saturn at 15 degrees Capricorn formed a nearly exact trine to his Sun at 14 degrees Taurus and a sextile to his Moon at 17 degrees Pisces. This created a harmonious web connecting Saturn's discipline and structure with his core identity and emotional nature.

In Denver, Michael experienced Saturn IC energy as deeply grounding. He finally felt capable of establishing emotional roots after years of restless wandering. The discipline came naturally rather than feeling forced or punishing. He renovated an old house methodically, taking genuine pleasure in the slow, careful work. His relationship with his aging parents matured into something authentic and satisfying. The emotional foundation he built in Denver felt solid, real, and sustainable.

The Saturn-Sun trine meant that Saturnian discipline supported rather than conflicted with his core identity. Building structure felt like expressing who he really was, not like forcing himself into someone else's expectations. The Saturn-Moon sextile meant that emotional security came through patience, boundaries, and mature limits rather than through spontaneity or endless permission. The harmonious aspects transformed what could have been restrictive Saturn energy into empowering, stabilizing influence.

Rachel: Saturn Square Venus, Opposite Mars

Rachel also relocated to a Saturn IC line, choosing Seattle based on career opportunities. Her natal Saturn at 8 degrees Libra squared her Venus at 10 degrees Cancer and opposed her Mars at 9 degrees Aries. This created a tense web connecting Saturn's restrictions with her capacity for pleasure and her assertive drive.

Rachel's experience in Seattle felt crushing rather than grounding. Every attempt to create emotional security seemed to require sacrificing what brought her joy. Her Venus-Saturn square manifested as feeling she had to choose between pleasure and responsibility, between what she wanted and what she should do. The Saturn-Mars opposition created constant internal conflict between pushing forward and holding back, between assertion and restraint.

Her home renovation projects felt like endless obligation rather than satisfying work. Her attempts to establish routines felt rigid and joyless. Relationships became heavy with unspoken expectations and resentment. After two years, Rachel relocated again, describing Seattle as the place where she learned that not every line that looks interesting on paper actually works for your particular chart.

The challenging aspects didn't mean Rachel was doing something wrong or that she failed to work with the energy correctly. They meant her natal Saturn web, when geographically activated, created more friction than flow. The same line that strengthened Michael restricted Rachel because their natal aspect patterns were fundamentally different.

Jennifer: Saturn Conjunct Neptune, Trine Pluto

Jennifer moved to Santa Fe on her Saturn IC line. Her natal Saturn at 22 degrees Sagittarius was conjunct Neptune at 24 degrees Sagittarius and trine Pluto at 21 degrees Leo. This created a complex web blending Saturn's structure with Neptune's dissolution and Pluto's transformation.

In Santa Fe, Jennifer experienced Saturn IC as spiritual discipline rather than either pure stability or pure restriction. The Saturn-Neptune conjunction meant structure and boundaries served mystical and creative purposes rather than purely practical ones. She established a meditation practice that required genuine commitment but opened profound inner experiences. Her home became a sanctuary for spiritual work, requiring maintenance and boundaries but supporting transcendent states.

The Saturn-Pluto trine added depth and transformative power to her structural efforts. Building her emotional foundation required confronting and releasing old patterns. Discipline became a vehicle for psychological regeneration rather than simply maintaining the status quo. The experience was neither easy like Michael's nor difficult like Rachel's. It was intense, meaningful, and ultimately transformative in ways that matched her unique natal configuration.

Three people. One line. Three completely different experiences, all determined by their natal aspect patterns. This is why understanding your aspect web is essential for sophisticated astrocartography work.

What Aspects Actually Are

Before we can work with aspects in astrocartography, we need clear understanding of what aspects are and how they function. If you're already fluent in aspect interpretation, this section will be review. If aspects are newer territory, pay close attention. This is the foundation for everything that follows.

Aspects as Angular Relationships

Aspects are geometric angles between planets as measured along the zodiac wheel. When two planets are certain specific numbers of degrees apart, they form an aspect. These aren't arbitrary numbers. They're based on dividing the 360-degree circle by various whole numbers, creating angles that seem to activate particular qualities of interaction between planetary energies.

The major aspects are conjunction (0 degrees, planets together), sextile (60 degrees, one sixth of the circle), square (90 degrees, one quarter of the circle), trine (120 degrees, one third of the circle), and opposition (180 degrees, planets opposite). Each angular relationship creates a different quality of interaction between the planetary energies involved.

Aspects have orbs, which means they don't have to be exactly precise to function. A trine doesn't stop working at 119 degrees and suddenly start at exactly 120 degrees. Most astrologers use orbs of 6 to 8 degrees for major aspects, meaning a trine can range from 112 degrees to 128 degrees and still count as a trine. Tighter orbs (closer to exact) generally create stronger, more obvious aspect manifestations. Wider orbs create subtler influences.

Harmonious Aspects: Trines and Sextiles

Trines and sextiles are traditionally called harmonious or easy aspects. This doesn't mean they're better than other aspects. It means the planetary energies flow together naturally, supporting rather than challenging each other. Things associated with these planetary combinations tend to come easily, require less conscious effort, and feel natural rather than forced.

Trines connect planets in the same element (fire to fire, earth to earth, air to air, water to water), creating a sense of natural compatibility. If your Venus trines your Jupiter, pleasure and expansion naturally support each other. Relationships feel fortunate. Aesthetic appreciation flows easily. Values and beliefs align harmoniously. The challenge with trines is sometimes they're so easy that you take them for granted or fail to develop their potential through conscious effort.

Sextiles connect planets in compatible elements (fire to air, earth to water), creating opportunities that require slight effort to activate but flow smoothly once engaged. If your Moon sextiles your Mercury, emotional understanding and mental processing cooperate naturally. You can talk about feelings. You can understand emotions intellectually. The potential is there, but unlike a trine, you need to consciously engage it.

Challenging Aspects: Squares and Oppositions

Squares and oppositions are traditionally called hard or challenging aspects. Again, this doesn't mean they're bad. It means the planetary energies create friction, tension, or conflict that requires conscious work to integrate. These aspects are often the source of the most growth and development in a chart because they can't be ignored. They demand attention, effort, and resolution.

Squares connect planets in different modes (cardinal, fixed, mutable) and incompatible elements. They create internal tension, a sense that two parts of yourself want different things. If your Sun squares your Saturn, your core identity and your sense of responsibility or limitation are in conflict. You might feel torn between self-expression and self-restraint, between shining and shrinking, between confidence and doubt. The friction can be uncomfortable, but it's also what drives development. You're forced to find ways to honor both energies rather than letting one dominate.

Oppositions place planets directly across the zodiac from each other, creating a polarity that needs balancing. If your Venus opposes your Mars, desire and assertion, receptivity and pursuit, feminine and masculine energies need integration. You might project one end of the polarity onto others, seeing them as too aggressive while you remain too passive, or vice versa. The work of an opposition is recognizing that both ends belong to you and finding ways to express both appropriately.

Conjunctions: Blended or Battling

Conjunctions place planets in the same sign at roughly the same degree. The energies are fused, operating as a single unit rather than as separate forces. Whether this feels harmonious or challenging depends on the nature of the planets involved. Venus conjunct Jupiter tends toward harmonious blending, easy expansion of pleasure and beauty. Mars conjunct Saturn tends toward tense combination, drive meeting restriction in ways that can be frustrating or disciplined depending on how you work with it.

In astrocartography, conjunctions are particularly powerful because activating one planet automatically activates the other. There's no separating them geographically. If you have Sun conjunct Mercury, your Sun line is also your Mercury line. Identity and communication activate simultaneously. This can be wonderfully cohesive or occasionally overwhelming depending on the planets involved and how they relate to the rest of your chart.

How This Changes Everything You Thought You Knew

Understanding natal aspects transforms astrocartography from generic planetary meanings to precise personal interpretation. You stop asking whether Venus lines are good and start asking what your Venus aspects are. You stop avoiding Saturn lines categorically and start evaluating whether your Saturn aspects create growth opportunities or unnecessary difficulty. You become more strategic, more informed, and more successful in choosing locations that actually work for your unique chart.

Questions That Change

Without aspect awareness, you ask simple questions. Should I move to Paris? Will my Jupiter line be good for my career? Is my Saturn line too challenging to visit? These questions assume planetary lines have universal meanings that apply to everyone similarly.

With aspect awareness, your questions become sophisticated. Paris is on my Venus Descendant line, and my Venus squares Pluto and trines Neptune. What kind of relationships am I likely to encounter there? My Jupiter line runs through Austin, and Jupiter trines my Sun but squares my Moon. Will career expansion come at the cost of emotional security? My Saturn line crosses Tokyo, and Saturn sextiles my Mercury but opposes my Mars. Will the discipline support my communication or frustrate my drive?

These more nuanced questions lead to more accurate predictions and better decision-making. You're not guessing based on generic interpretations. You're analyzing based on your actual natal configuration.

The Strategic Advantage

Once you understand aspect activation, you gain strategic advantage in timing and location decisions. You know which lines will likely work smoothly for you based on harmonious aspects and which lines require more conscious work due to challenging aspects. You can match your developmental needs to appropriate line activations. If you're ready to work through Venus-Saturn relationship patterns, you might choose to spend time on a Venus line during a Saturn transit, deliberately activating the challenging aspect for growth. If you need ease and recovery, you choose lines with harmonious aspects during supportive transits.

This level of sophistication is rare in astrocartography practice. Most people work with lines in isolation, missing the aspect layer entirely. Those who understand aspect activation have access to far more precise, powerful, and personalized location astrology. This is your advantage. This is what this book teaches.

In the next chapter, we'll learn exactly how to map your unique aspect web, identifying which planets connect to which other planets through which aspects. This becomes your personal reference guide for the rest of the book and for the rest of your astrocartography practice. Every decision about location, timing, and strategy will flow from understanding your web's unique structure.

Chapter Two

Mapping Your Unique Aspect Web

I'll never forget the day a client called me, confused and frustrated. She'd been living on her Venus line for six months, and it wasn't working the way she expected. "You said Venus lines bring love and beauty," she said. "But I feel..." She paused, searching for words. "Complicated."

That's when I realized I'd given her incomplete information. I'd told her about her Venus line, but I hadn't taught her how to map her Venus web. I hadn't shown her that her Venus squared Pluto and opposed Mars, creating layers of intensity and transformation that no generic "Venus brings love" interpretation could capture. I'd sent her to Barcelona expecting ease and romance when her chart was actually set up for deep psychological work around desire, power, and relating.

That conversation changed how I teach astrocartography. You can't work strategically with your aspect web until you know what that web actually looks like. This chapter shows you exactly how to map yours—not as abstract theory, but as practical reference you'll use for every astrocartography decision you make from this point forward.

We'll work through this systematically, planet by planet, identifying aspects with clear orbs and noting whether they're harmonious, challenging, or neutral. By the end of this chapter, you'll have your personal aspect web mapped comprehensively. You'll know exactly which planets activate when you travel to any line on your astrocartography map.

What You Need Before You Start

You'll need your natal chart with exact planetary positions and an aspect grid showing the angles between planets. Most astrology software and websites provide this automatically. I like to use Astro.com, but Astro-seek.com or astro.com work just as well. Your free natal chart will include an aspect grid at the bottom showing all major aspects between planets.

Reading an Aspect Grid

An aspect grid is a table showing planets along both axes. Where planets intersect in the grid, you'll see symbols indicating aspects (if any exist). The symbols typically used are a small circle with a dot for conjunction, a star or asterisk for sextile, a small square for square, a triangle for trine, and two circles or a straight line for opposition. Different software uses slightly different symbols, but they're usually labeled clearly.

The grid will also show the orb, the exact number of degrees between planets. A Venus-Jupiter trine might show as 118 degrees 35 minutes, meaning they're not exactly 120 degrees apart but close enough to count as a trine. Pay attention to tight orbs (within 3 degrees) as these create the strongest, most obvious manifestations. Wider orbs (4 to 8 degrees) still count but express more subtly.

Which Aspects to Track

For astrocartography purposes, focus on the five major aspects: conjunction, sextile, square, trine, and opposition. These are the aspects that create clear, consistent effects when geographically activated. Minor aspects like quincunxes, semi-sextiles, and quintiles do matter in natal chart interpretation but are subtler in astrocartography activation. If you want to track them eventually, you can, but start with the major five.

Use an orb of 8 degrees maximum for trines and oppositions, 6 degrees for squares and sextiles, and up to 10 degrees for conjunctions (since conjunctions are the strongest aspect). Tighter is better. An aspect with a 1-degree orb will be far more obvious than one with a 7-degree orb, but both technically count.

Creating Your Aspect Web Document

Now we'll create a practical reference document organizing all your aspects by the planetary line they affect. This becomes your roadmap for every astrocartography decision. I recommend creating a simple document or spreadsheet with the following structure for each planet in your chart.

Sun Aspect Web

List your Sun's zodiac position and degree. Then list every aspect your Sun makes to other planets, noting the aspect type, the other planet involved, and the exact orb. For example: Sun at 13 Aries. Sun trine Jupiter (118 degrees, orb 2 degrees). Sun square Saturn (88 degrees, orb 5 degrees). Sun sextile Neptune (58 degrees, orb 5 degrees).

This tells you that whenever you're on your Sun line or when transits cross your Sun line, you're simultaneously activating Jupiter (harmoniously), Saturn (with tension), and Neptune (with opportunity). All four bodies wake up together. Understanding this web explains why your Sun line experiences are more complex than just pure solar expression.

Moon Aspect Web

Follow the same process for your Moon. List its position and every aspect it makes. The Moon typically has more aspects than most planets because it moves so quickly through the zodiac at birth, it frequently forms aspects to multiple planets within the few hours of birth.

Your Moon aspects are particularly important because the Moon represents emotional security, instinctive responses, and comfort. When you're on your Moon line, how your Moon aspects other planets determines whether you feel emotionally safe (Moon trine Venus), emotionally intense (Moon square Pluto), emotionally expansive (Moon trine Jupiter), or emotionally restricted (Moon square Saturn).

Repeat for All Planets

Create the same structure for Mercury, Venus, Mars, Jupiter, Saturn, Uranus, Neptune, and Pluto. Yes, this takes time. Yes, it's worth it. This document becomes your personal astrocartography bible. You'll reference it constantly when evaluating locations, planning trips, or understanding why certain places feel particular ways.

Some planets will have many aspects. Others will have few or none. A planet with no aspects (unaspected) operates more purely and independently, which can be either liberating or isolating depending on the planet and your relationship to that planetary energy. Venus with no aspects expresses pure Venusian qualities without modification from other planetary influences.

Understanding Aspect Strength and Priority

Not all aspects in your web carry equal weight. Tighter orbs create stronger, more consistent manifestations. Aspects involving personal planets (Sun, Moon, Mercury, Venus, Mars) feel more immediate and obvious than aspects involving outer planets. Aspects to your chart angles (Ascendant, Midheaven, IC, Descendant) are particularly powerful even though angles aren't planets.

Orb Tightness

An aspect with a 0 to 2-degree orb is applying (planets moving toward exact) or separating (planets moving past exact) and will be extremely obvious in manifestation. You'll feel this aspect clearly and consistently when the line is activated. An aspect with a 2 to 4-degree orb is also quite strong and reliable. An aspect with a 4 to 6-degree orb is moderate, present but not always obvious. An aspect with a 6 to 8-degree orb is subtle and may only manifest under certain conditions or in certain areas of life.

When evaluating whether to travel to a particular line, prioritize tight-orb aspects in your decision-making. If your Venus trines Jupiter with a 1-degree orb and squares Saturn with a 7-degree orb, the Jupiter influence will likely dominate your Venus line experience. The Saturn square will be there, but more as background than foreground.

Personal vs. Outer Planet Aspects

Aspects between personal planets (Sun, Moon, Mercury, Venus, Mars) feel immediate, personal, and within your conscious control. Sun square Mars creates internal tension you experience directly and can work with consciously. Aspects involving social planets (Jupiter, Saturn) operate at the level of opportunity and structure, sometimes feeling more external than internal. Aspects involving outer planets (Uranus, Neptune, Pluto) operate at transpersonal, generational, or unconscious levels, sometimes taking years to fully understand.

For astrocartography, this means personal planet aspects tend to manifest more quickly and obviously when you activate a line. Outer planet aspects may unfold more slowly, reveal themselves over time, or operate through circumstances and other people rather than as

THE POWER OF PLACE: MASTER 17

direct personal experiences. Both matter, but personal planet aspects are typically easier to work with consciously.

Working Example: Mapping Sarah's Venus Web

Let's walk through a complete example using a fictional chart to demonstrate the mapping process. Sarah's Venus is at 18 degrees Libra. Looking at her aspect grid, she identifies the following aspects:

Venus trine Jupiter at 19 degrees Gemini, with a 1-degree orb. This is an extremely tight harmonious aspect. Venus square Saturn at 20 degrees Capricorn, with a 2-degree orb. This is a moderately tight challenging aspect. Venus sextile Mars at 16 degrees Leo, with a 2-degree orb. This is a moderately tight harmonious aspect. Venus trine Neptune at 17 degrees Aquarius, with a 1-degree orb. This is an extremely tight harmonious aspect.

Sarah's Venus web includes four significant aspects, three harmonious and one challenging. When she travels to her Venus lines (Ascendant, Descendant, IC, or Midheaven), all five bodies activate: Venus itself, Jupiter (harmony expansion), Saturn (challenge restriction), Mars (energy desire), and Neptune (spirituality illusion).

The predominance of harmonious aspects (trine Jupiter, sextile Mars, trine Neptune) suggests Sarah's Venus lines will generally feel supportive, particularly in relationships, pleasure, and aesthetic experiences. However, the Venus-Saturn square introduces a complicating factor. She may experience tension between desire and duty, between what feels good and what feels responsible, between pleasure and restriction. The tight Neptune trine adds a spiritual or creative dimension but also potential for idealization or confusion in relationships.

This analysis is far more sophisticated than simply saying Venus lines bring love and beauty. It accounts for how Sarah's unique Venus connects to the rest of her chart, creating a specific, personalized prediction about what Venus line activation will actually feel like for her rather than for some theoretical generic person.

You'll follow this same process for all ten planets in your chart (or nine if you don't work with Pluto), creating a comprehensive web map that becomes your permanent astrocartography reference guide. In the next chapter, we'll explore exactly how transits interact with these natal aspect webs, adding the crucial timing dimension to geographic activation.

Chapter Three

When Transits Meet Your Aspect Web

Two clients came to me in the same month, both planning moves to their Moon lines during Saturn transits. On paper, the astrology looked identical—Saturn crossing the Moon, a notoriously challenging transit for emotional security and home life. Traditional interpretation said both should expect the same experience: restrictions, tests, emotional heaviness, difficult family dynamics.

I looked at their natal aspects. The first client had Moon trine Venus and sextile Jupiter. The second had the Moon square Mars and opposite Pluto. Same transit, same line, completely different natal webs. I knew their experiences would be nothing alike.

The first client sent me updates throughout her Saturn transit. Yes, she faced challenges around home and family. Yes, Saturn demanded maturity and responsibility. But her relationships remained supportive. People showed up for her. The emotional difficulty felt workable, even growth-producing. The second client's experience was far more intense. Every challenge felt magnified. Anger erupted unpredictably. Deep psychological material surfaced constantly. After eight months, he relocated again.

Same transit. Same line. Completely different outcomes, all explained by their natal aspect webs. This is what changed everything for me about timing astrocartography travel. Understanding your natal aspects isn't enough. You also need to understand how transits interact with those aspects, because that interaction determines whether a challenging transit creates growth or crisis, whether a harmonious transit brings ease or missed opportunity.

Single-Point Activation vs. Web Activation

Traditional transit interpretation treats each transit as activating a single natal planet in isolation. Transiting Jupiter crosses your natal Sun? Expect expansion, opportunity, confidence. Transiting Saturn crosses your natal Venus? Expect relationship challenges, commitment questions, values testing. This isn't wrong, but it's incomplete. It ignores the web of connections radiating from each planet.

The Isolation Model

In the isolation model, each transit activates only the planet it touches. Your chart has ten planets sitting in different houses, different signs, doing their separate things. When a transiting planet crosses one of them, that one planet lights up temporarily. The transit comes, does its thing, and leaves. Simple, linear, straightforward.

This model works reasonably well for understanding basic transit effects, but it fails to account for the interconnected nature of your psyche. You don't have ten separate planetary drives operating independently. You have a unified consciousness in which different drives, needs, and energies constantly interact through the aspects between your natal planets. When one planet gets activated by a transit or by geographic location, the activation doesn't stop there. It ripples through the web.

The Web Model

In the web model, transits activate not just single planets but entire aspect patterns. When transiting Saturn crosses your natal Moon, it simultaneously activates every planet that aspects your Moon. If your Moon trines Pluto, Saturn activates both Moon and Pluto. If your Moon squares Jupiter, Saturn activates Moon and Jupiter. If your Moon trines Pluto and squares Jupiter simultaneously, Saturn activates all three bodies at once.

This creates far more complex experiences than simple Saturn-Moon interpretation suggests. You're not just experiencing Saturn testing your emotional security (Saturn-Moon). You're experiencing Saturn testing your emotional security while simultaneously activating your capacity for depth and transformation (Moon-Pluto trine) and creating tension between emotional needs and expansive desires (Moon-Jupiter square). Three different dynamics operating simultaneously, all triggered by one transit crossing one line.

The web model explains why the same transit feels completely different to different people. It's not the same transit. It's the same transiting planet crossing the same natal planet, but activating completely different webs depending on each person's unique aspect structure. Your Saturn crossing your Moon is fundamentally different from someone else's Saturn crossing their Moon if your Moon aspects are different from theirs.

Simultaneous vs. Sequential Activation

When a transit activates your aspect web, all the aspected planets wake up at once. This simultaneous activation creates experiences that blend and interact in real time rather than happening one after another. Understanding the difference between simultaneous and sequential activation helps you predict how complex the experience will be and what kind of integration work you'll need to do.

Simultaneous Activation: Everything at Once

When you're on your Moon line and transiting Saturn crosses it, your Moon doesn't activate first, followed by planets that aspect it. They all activate together, creating a field of combined energies operating simultaneously. If your Moon trines Venus and squares Mars, you experience Saturnian restriction on emotional security (Saturn-Moon) combined with ease in relationships (Moon-Venus trine) and tension in assertion (Moon-Mars square) all happening at the same moment.

This simultaneity can feel confusing or contradictory if you're not aware of the web structure. You might feel both supported and frustrated, both opened and closed, both flowing and stuck, all within the same experience. The web model helps you understand these seeming contradictions as different aspect threads activating together rather than as random chaos or mixed signals from the universe.

Lisa's Experience: Moon-Venus-Saturn Web

Lisa traveled to her Moon IC line in Charleston during a Saturn transit crossing her natal Moon. Her natal Moon at 25 degrees Cancer formed a trine to Venus at 21 degrees Pisces and a square to Saturn at 27 degrees Aries. When transiting Saturn at 25 degrees Cancer crossed her Moon line, it activated all three bodies simultaneously.

The Moon-Saturn conjunction by transit brought challenges to her emotional foundation and sense of home security, exactly as traditional Saturn-Moon interpretation predicts. However, the simultaneous activation of her Moon-Venus trine softened the experience significantly. She felt restrictions and demands around home and family, but relationships remained sources of comfort and support. Her capacity for pleasure and beauty didn't disappear under Saturn's pressure. The trine kept flowing.

The natal Moon-Saturn square added another layer. Because her Moon and Saturn already have a challenging relationship in her natal chart, the transit of Saturn to her Moon felt somewhat familiar rather than shocking or devastating. She'd been working with Moon-Saturn tension her entire life. The transit intensified patterns she already knew how to navigate, rather than introducing entirely foreign restrictions.

The result was complex but workable. Charleston demanded maturity around home and family during this period, but Lisa's Venus trine kept relationships supportive, and her natal Moon-Saturn square meant she had existing skills for handling Saturnian emotional restrictions. All three dynamics operated simultaneously, creating an experience far more nuanced than simple Saturn crosses Moon interpretation would suggest.

Sequential Activation: One After Another

Sequential activation occurs when multiple transits cross different points in your aspect web at different times. This creates an unfolding story rather than a single complex moment. If Saturn transits your Moon in June, then transiting Jupiter trines your Moon (and thus aspects your natal Moon-Pluto trine) in September, you experience two distinct phases of Moon web activation separated by time.

Sequential activation is generally easier to work with than simultaneous activation because you can focus on one dynamic at a time, integrate it, and then move to the next. Simultaneous activation requires holding multiple contradictory or complementary energies at once, which can be overwhelming. Sequential activation gives you breathing room between different web activations.

The Ripple Effect: How One Transit Activates Multiple Planets

When a transit crosses a planetary line, it creates a ripple effect through your aspect web. The more aspects a planet has, the wider the ripple. A planet with six aspects creates a six-body activation when transited. A planet with two aspects creates a three-body activation. Understanding this ripple helps you predict the scope and intensity of any transit-line combination.

Marcus's Jupiter Transit: Four-Body Activation

Marcus planned a three-month stay in Berlin, which fell on his Sun Midheaven line. He timed the trip to coincide with transiting Jupiter crossing his natal Sun, expecting career expansion and professional recognition. What he didn't account for was his Sun's extensive aspect web. His natal Sun at 12 degrees Gemini formed a trine to Saturn at 14 degrees Aquarius, a square to Neptune at 15 degrees Pisces, and a sextile to Mars at 10 degrees Leo.

When transiting Jupiter crossed his Sun at 12 degrees Gemini, it didn't just expand Sun themes. It simultaneously activated Saturn (structure, discipline, limitation), Neptune (vision, confusion, spirituality), and Mars (drive, action, assertion). Four bodies lit up at once, creating a far more complex experience than Jupiter-Sun expansion alone would suggest.

The Sun-Saturn trine meant professional expansion required solid structure and realistic planning. Jupiter's optimism had to work within Saturnian constraints. The Sun-Neptune square brought both inspiring vision and confusing illusions about his professional path. The Sun-Mars sextile provided energetic drive to pursue opportunities but required conscious effort to activate fully.

Berlin during this period brought Marcus tremendous opportunities (Jupiter-Sun), but only those built on realistic foundations succeeded (Sun-Saturn trine). He had inspiring visions about his career direction (Sun-Neptune square) that required careful discernment to separate genuine intuition from wishful thinking. His drive and energy remained high (Sun-Mars sextile), giving him the capacity to pursue multiple opportunities simultaneously.

Had Marcus understood his Sun aspect web before traveling, he could have prepared for the complexity. He would have known to build structure into his expansion plans, to question his visions carefully before acting on them, and to consciously activate his Mars sextile through decisive action. Instead, the four-body activation caught him by surprise, creating both more opportunity and more confusion than he expected.

Harmonious Aspects Soften Challenging Transits

One of the most practically useful insights from understanding transit-web interaction is that harmonious natal aspects can significantly soften challenging transits. When a difficult transit crosses a line, but that planet has supportive aspects to other planets, those supportive aspects continue flowing even while the transit creates challenges. This creates resilience and resources that traditional transit interpretation often misses.

Diana's Saturn Transit With Support

Diana relocated to her Venus Descendant line in Barcelona just as transiting Saturn was approaching her natal Venus. Traditional interpretation predicted relationship restrictions, delayed partnerships, and tests of values. Diana almost cancelled the move based on this timing. However, analysis of her Venus aspect web revealed significant supportive structures.

Her natal Venus at 8 degrees Scorpio formed a trine to Jupiter at 9 degrees Cancer and a sextile to Neptune at 7 degrees Capricorn. When transiting Saturn crossed her Venus in Barcelona, yes, it brought

Saturn-Venus themes of commitment, limitation, and serious relationship questions. But simultaneously, her Venus-Jupiter trine kept flowing, maintaining opportunities for connection, generosity, and fortunate relationship encounters. Her Venus-Neptune sextile continued offering spiritual depth and romantic idealism that could be consciously accessed.

The result was that Saturn's transit matured her relationships without crushing her capacity for love. She met someone during this period who brought both serious commitment potential and genuine joy. The relationship required work and patience (Saturn), but it wasn't grim or heavy. The Jupiter trine kept things fortunate and expansive. The Neptune sextile added spiritual connection and creative partnership. Saturn provided structure for these harmonious energies rather than simply restricting them.

Diana's experience illustrates a crucial principle: challenging transits to planets with harmonious natal aspects are almost always more workable than challenging transits to planets with challenging natal aspects. The natal harmonious aspects provide ongoing support, resources, and ease even while the transit creates tests and demands.

Challenging Aspects Intensify Difficult Transits

The opposite is equally true: challenging natal aspects can intensify already difficult transits, creating periods of maximum pressure that require careful consideration before committing to travel or relocation. This doesn't mean you should never be on a line during a challenging transit if that planet has challenging natal aspects. It means you should go in with eyes open, adequate support systems, and realistic expectations.

Robert's Saturn Transit Without Support

Robert relocated to Denver on his Moon IC line during a Saturn transit to his natal Moon. His natal Moon at 24 degrees Pisces formed a square to Mars at 22 degrees Gemini and an opposition to Pluto at 26 degrees Virgo. No harmonious aspects softened his Moon. When transiting Saturn crossed his Moon, it activated an already tense natal configuration.

The Saturn transit brought expected emotional restrictions and challenges around home and security. But simultaneously, the Moon-Mars square intensified, creating explosive emotional reactions and frustrated anger he couldn't quite express appropriately. The Moon-Pluto opposition activated, bringing up deep psychological material, power struggles with family, and feelings of being controlled or manipulated.

Denver during this period felt overwhelming. Every challenge felt magnified. Robert's emotional foundation wasn't just being tested by Saturn. It was being tested while his anger flared unpredictably (Moon-Mars square) and his deepest fears and control issues surfaced constantly (Moon-Pluto opposition). The lack of harmonious aspects in his Moon web meant there were no easy, flowing channels for release or support.

After eight months, Robert relocated again. He didn't regret the Denver experience. It forced significant psychological growth. But he wished he'd understood before moving that the timing would be as intense as it turned out to be. Had he known, he would have either delayed the move until Saturn finished transiting his Moon, or he would have ensured stronger support systems were in place before relocating.

Robert's experience demonstrates that challenging transits to planets with challenging natal aspects create peak intensity periods. These can be incredibly valuable for growth, but they're not times to expect ease or comfort. If you choose to relocate during such periods, do so with full awareness of what you're signing up for.

Practical Implications for Timing

Understanding transit-web activation completely transforms your timing strategies for travel and relocation. You stop making decisions based solely on whether a transit is traditionally good or challenging and start evaluating whether that transit will activate harmonious or challenging natal aspects in your web. This level of sophistication dramatically improves your outcomes.

Best Times to Travel to Each Line

For any planetary line you're considering, look at upcoming transits to that planet over the next two to three years. Then evaluate those transits not just by the transiting planet's nature but by what aspects they'll activate in your natal web. A Jupiter transit crossing your Saturn line might seem paradoxical, expansion meeting restriction. But if your natal Saturn trines your Sun, Jupiter transiting Saturn will expand structured, disciplined solar expression. That could be excellent timing for career development.

The optimal timing is when harmonious transits cross lines whose natal planets have harmonious aspects. This creates multiple layers of support, flow, and ease. The challenging timing is when challenging transits cross lines whose natal planets have challenging aspects. This creates multiple layers of friction, tension, and difficulty. The workable timing is mixed combinations: challenging transits with harmonious natal aspects, or harmonious transits with challenging natal aspects.

When to Avoid or Embrace Intensity

Sometimes you want to avoid intensity. You're recovering from crisis, you need stability and ease, or you're at capacity with other life challenges. During these periods, choose lines with harmonious natal aspects during harmonious transits. Create every possible layer of support and flow. This isn't escapism. It's intelligent self-care and strategic recovery.

Other times you're ready for intensity. You're at a transformation point, you have adequate support, you're willing to do deep work, or you're seeking maximum growth even at the cost of comfort. During these periods, you might deliberately choose lines with challenging natal aspects during challenging transits. This creates concentrated growth experiences. Just make sure you're choosing intensity consciously rather than stumbling into it unprepared.

The key word is consciousness. Make informed choices based on understanding your natal web and current transits rather than hoping for the best or fearing the worst without adequate information. In the following chapters, we'll examine specific aspect combinations in detail, giving you precise frameworks for evaluating every possible natal aspect pattern and how it modifies line experiences and transit timing.

Chapter Four

Harmonious Aspects: Trines and Sextiles in Your Web

I remember watching a client's face change as I explained her Venus trine Jupiter. She'd been living on her Venus line for a year, confused about why relationships and money seemed to flow so effortlessly when she'd been told that personal growth required struggle. "Is something wrong with me?" she asked. "Should I be working harder?"

Nothing was wrong. She had simply activated one of the most fortunate aspects in astrology. Venus trine Jupiter creates a channel where pleasure and expansion support each other naturally, where what feels good also leads to growth, where ease doesn't mean you're doing it wrong—it means you're working with your chart's natural flow instead of against it.

This is what trines and sextiles do. Trines and sextiles are the aspects that make certain lines feel like coming home, like finding your natural element, like suddenly everything flows with minimal effort. These harmonious aspects don't eliminate challenges entirely, but they create channels of ease, support, and natural talent that transform line experiences from work into play, from struggle into grace. Understanding how harmonious aspects modify your lines helps you identify which locations will support you most naturally and which times to travel for recovery, integration, and effortless expansion.

This chapter explores exactly how trines and sextiles function in astrocartography, examines the subtle differences between these two harmonious aspects, and provides detailed examples of how they manifest across different planetary combinations. By the end, you'll understand why some lines feel like instant belonging while others require more conscious activation.

How Trines Create Flow

Trines connect planets in the same element, creating a sense that different parts of your psyche speak the same language and naturally support each other. Fire trines fire, creating spontaneous action and enthusiasm. Earth trines earth, creating practical manifestation and grounded stability. Air trines air, creating mental connection and communicative ease. Water trines water, creating emotional understanding and intuitive flow.

When you activate a planetary line and that planet has trines to other planets, those trines continue flowing effortlessly even when other factors create challenges. The trine is your fallback position, your reliable source of support, your automatic advantage. You don't have to work to activate a trine. It's just there, operating naturally in the background like breathing or heartbeat.

Maria's Moon-Jupiter Trine on Moon Line

Maria relocated to Portland on her Moon IC line. Her natal Moon at 8 degrees Scorpio formed an exact trine to Jupiter at 8 degrees Pisces, both water signs creating a flowing, intuitive connection between emotional security and expansion. The trine was tight, less than one degree orb, meaning its influence was powerful and consistent.

In Portland, Maria experienced her Moon line not as restriction or intense emotional work but as emotional abundance and ease. Home felt naturally expansive rather than confining. Family relationships that had been complicated in other locations became generous, forgiving, and growth-oriented. Her intuition operated at a high level, providing reliable guidance without conscious effort. Emotional security came through spiritual practice and philosophical understanding rather than through controlling circumstances.

The Moon-Jupiter trine meant that emotional needs and expansive opportunities naturally aligned. Maria didn't have to choose between feeling safe and growing. She didn't have to sacrifice security for adventure or vice versa. The two worked together automatically. When she needed emotional comfort, Jupiter's optimism and faith were right there. When she wanted to expand, her Moon provided instinctive timing about when expansion felt safe versus reckless.

After two years in Portland, Maria described the experience as feeling like her emotional life had been given permission to be easy for the first time. The Moon-Jupiter trine didn't eliminate all challenges, but it provided a foundation of flow that made challenges workable rather than overwhelming. This is how trines function in astrocartography. They create ease that becomes your reliable home base.

Element-Specific Trine Dynamics

While all trines create flow, the element involved fundamentally shapes how that flow manifests and what shadows emerge. Understanding elemental differences in trine expression allows more nuanced prediction and strategic planning.

Fire Trines (Aries, Leo, Sagittarius)

Fire trines create spontaneous enthusiasm, confident initiative, and natural leadership. When you activate lines involving Fire trines, creative inspiration flows abundantly and bold action feels natural rather than forced. The shadow involves burning too brightly without sustainable fuel, starting without finishing, or mistaking ease for mastery.

Sun trine Mars in Fire signs creates unstoppable initiative and courageous self-expression. On Sun lines, you lead naturally and inspire others through authentic enthusiasm. On Mars lines, your actions align with core identity without internal conflict. The challenge: distinguishing confident action from reckless impulsivity. Fire trines can make everything feel like a good idea in the moment.

Example: Daniel has Sun in Aries trine Mars in Sagittarius. On his Sun line in Denver, he launched three businesses in two years, each with tremendous initial success fueled by his natural Fire trine confidence. However, two failed because he moved to the next exciting venture before establishing sustainable systems. The Fire trine provided endless initiative but no patience for maintenance. He learned to consciously add Earth element (hiring detail-oriented managers) to channel Fire flow productively.

Earth Trines (Taurus, Virgo, Capricorn)

Earth trines create practical manifestation, steady accumulation, and grounded achievement. When you activate lines involving Earth trines, material success flows naturally and sustainable structures build without excessive struggle. The shadow involves excessive focus on security, resistance to necessary change, or confusing material success with meaningful fulfillment.

Venus trine Saturn in Earth signs creates natural wealth-building capacity and aesthetic refinement that appreciates in value. On Venus lines, relationships and resources stabilize easily. On Saturn lines, discipline feels rewarding rather than punishing. The challenge: becoming so comfortable with material security that spiritual or emotional growth stagnates.

Example: Patricia has Venus in Taurus trine Saturn in Virgo. On her Venus line in Portland, she built substantial real estate holdings and a profitable organic farm with seemingly effortless success. The Earth trine made material manifestation natural. However, after five years, she felt empty despite financial abundance. The Earth trine had created sustainable wealth but no deeper meaning. She added Water element practices (meditation, emotional depth work) to balance material focus with spiritual development.

Air Trines (Gemini, Libra, Aquarius)

Air trines create intellectual brilliance, social grace, and communicative facility. When you activate lines involving Air trines, ideas flow abundantly and connections form effortlessly. The shadow involves living in the head rather than the body, intellectual understanding without emotional integration, or scattered mental energy across too many interests.

Mercury trine Venus in Air signs creates natural charm, persuasive communication, and aesthetic intelligence. On Mercury lines, writing and speaking flow beautifully. On Venus lines, relationships develop through intellectual affinity and elegant conversation. The challenge: confusing clever words for genuine feeling or avoiding emotional depth through constant mental activity.

Example: Marcus has Mercury in Gemini trine Venus in Aquarius. On his Mercury line in San Francisco, he became a celebrated writer and networked brilliantly in tech circles. The Air trine made intellectual work and social connection effortless. Friends noted he lived entirely in his mind, rarely feeling or embodying experience. After a relationship ended due to emotional unavailability, he began intensive therapy and embodiment practices, adding Water and Earth elements to balance Air brilliance with depth and presence.

Water Trines (Cancer, Scorpio, Pisces)

Water trines create emotional depth, psychic sensitivity, and spiritual connection. When you activate lines involving Water trines, intuition operates reliably and emotional understanding flows naturally. The shadow involves emotional overwhelm, boundary dissolution, or using sensitivity as excuse for avoiding practical action and material responsibility.

Moon trine Neptune in Water signs creates profound emotional-spiritual integration and artistic sensitivity. On Moon lines, home becomes sanctuary for mystical experience. On Neptune lines, spiritual practice feels emotionally nourishing rather than escapist. The challenge: drowning in emotion without clarity, or confusing psychic sensitivity with practical wisdom.

Example: Lisa has Moon in Cancer trine Neptune in Pisces. On her Moon line in Santa Fe, she accessed profound spiritual states and created deeply moving artwork. The Water trine made emotional-spiritual flow natural. However, she couldn't maintain employment, pay bills, or establish boundaries with needy people. The Water trine provided emotional-spiritual genius but no practical grounding. She learned business skills and established firm schedules, adding Earth and Fire elements to channel Water depth sustainably.

The Double Trine Effect

When a planet has trines to multiple other planets, activating that line creates multiple channels of flow simultaneously. This double or triple trine effect can feel almost magical in its ease, though it also carries the risk of taking advantages for granted or failing to develop skills because everything comes too easily.

James's Grand Trine Experience

James had natal Venus at 15 degrees Gemini forming trines to both Saturn at 17 degrees Aquarius and Neptune at 14 degrees Libra. All three planets in air signs, creating a grand trine focused on mental connection, aesthetic refinement, and structured creativity. When he relocated to Paris on his Venus Descendant line, all three planets activated their flowing relationships simultaneously.

Relationships in Paris felt naturally structured yet romantic, practical yet idealistic. The Venus-Saturn trine brought committed partnerships without heaviness, discipline in relationship without coldness. The Venus-Neptune trine added spiritual connection and creative collaboration without confusion or dissolution. The grand trine in air meant communication flowed effortlessly in relationships, creative projects had both vision and structure, and social connections developed easily through intellectual affinity.

The challenge James faced was complacency. Things went so smoothly in Paris that he sometimes failed to appreciate what he had or to consciously develop relationship skills. The grand trine created such natural ease that he occasionally coasted rather than growing. This is the shadow side of harmonious aspects. They can create such smooth conditions that you don't build strength or capacity through challenge.

Orb Considerations in Harmonious Aspects

The tightness of an aspect's orb significantly affects its manifestation in astrocartography. Tight orbs (0-3 degrees) create consistent, reliable flow. Wide orbs (6-10 degrees) create sporadic or conditional ease that requires more conscious activation.

Tight Orbs (0-3 degrees)

Exact or near-exact trines and sextiles operate like precision instruments, providing consistent support regardless of circumstances. These aspects become core personality features that you can rely on in any location. When you activate a line involving a tight harmonious aspect, the flow is immediately obvious and powerfully present.

Example: Rachel has Sun at 12 degrees Leo trine Moon at 12 degrees Sagittarius (exact 0-degree orb). This precise alignment creates unwavering integration between identity and emotions. On any Sun or Moon line, she experiences this fundamental harmony. The exactness means the flow never wavers—it's a permanent advantage in her chart that geography amplifies but doesn't create.

Wide Orbs (6-10 degrees)

Wider harmonious aspects provide potential support that manifests conditionally. You might experience the flow strongly during supportive transits or life periods, then barely notice it during challenging times. These aspects require more conscious activation and work best when you're already in good condition rather than during crisis.

Example: Thomas has Venus at 15 degrees Libra trine Jupiter at 24 degrees Aquarius (9-degree orb). This wide trine provides genuine support, but inconsistently. On his Venus line in Paris, he experienced the Venus-Jupiter flow strongly during Jupiter transits to his Venus or when his overall life was going well. During Saturn transits or stressful periods, the wide trine barely registered. He learned to consciously activate it through gratitude practices and generous acts, bringing the latent flow into manifestation.

How Sextiles Create Opportunity

Sextiles connect planets in compatible but not identical elements, creating opportunities that require slight conscious effort to activate but flow smoothly once engaged. Fire sextiles air, action energizes ideas. Earth sextiles water, practical resources support emotional flow. Unlike trines which operate automatically, sextiles offer potential that needs to be recognized and claimed.

In astrocartography, sextiles modify line experiences by providing accessible resources and opportunities that won't necessarily manifest unless you reach for them. A sextile is like having a door available that you still need to choose to walk through. The door is easy to open, but you have to notice it and decide to use it.

Carlos's Mars-Mercury Sextile on Mars Line

Carlos moved to Austin on his Mars Midheaven line to launch his technology consulting business. His natal Mars at 22 degrees Leo formed a sextile to Mercury at 21 degrees Libra. Fire sextile air, action supporting communication, assertiveness enhancing articulation. The sextile had a 1-degree orb, tight enough to be reliable but requiring conscious activation.

In Austin, Carlos's Mars line brought the expected entrepreneurial energy, drive, and courage to build his business. But the Mars-Mercury sextile added a crucial dimension that wouldn't have been there with Mars alone. When he consciously engaged his communication skills, his assertiveness became persuasive rather than aggressive. When he actively used his strategic thinking, his drive found productive channels rather than scattering.

The sextile didn't operate automatically. Carlos had to notice opportunities to combine action with communication, to use words as tools for his entrepreneurial drive. When he ignored the sextile and operated on pure Mars energy, he pushed too hard, burned bridges, or moved too fast without adequate planning. When he consciously activated the Mercury sextile, everything flowed. His pitches to clients were energetic and clear. His business decisions combined gut instinct with rational analysis. His leadership style was both decisive and articulate.

After three years in Austin, Carlos understood that the Mars-Mercury sextile was his secret weapon for business success, but only when he remembered to use it. Unlike a trine which would have made communication effortless, the sextile required him to consciously integrate talking and acting, thinking and doing. This conscious integration ultimately built skills that made him a more effective entrepreneur than pure Mars drive would have.

Sextiles as Skill Builders

The requirement that sextiles be consciously activated makes them excellent for skill development and capacity building. Unlike trines which can create talent without effort, sextiles create talent through conscious practice. You get good at integrating the planetary energies because you have to actively do it repeatedly. This builds genuine competence that becomes reliable over time.

For astrocartography purposes, this means lines involving sextiles are excellent for developmental periods when you're ready to consciously build skills rather than simply enjoying natural talents. If you have Sun sextile Venus and you travel to your Sun line, you can develop genuine charm, social grace, and aesthetic sensitivity by consciously integrating these energies. The opportunity is there. The ease is available. You just have to choose to engage it.

Planetary Combinations: Common Harmonious Aspects

Different planetary combinations create different flavors of harmonious flow. Understanding how specific planets work together through trines and sextiles helps you predict exactly what kind of ease or opportunity each line will offer when activated.

Sun-Moon Harmonious Aspects

Sun trine Moon or Sun sextile Moon creates natural alignment between conscious identity and emotional needs, between who you're trying to become and what makes you feel secure. On Sun lines, this manifests as confidence that doesn't sacrifice emotional authenticity. On Moon lines, this manifests as emotional security that supports rather than undermines personal growth. The integration of masculine and feminine, doing and being, expression and receptivity flows naturally.

Venus-Jupiter Harmonious Aspects

Venus trine Jupiter or Venus sextile Jupiter is often called the luckiest aspect in astrology, and for good reason. It expands pleasure, attracts generosity, and creates fortune in relationships and resources. On Venus lines, this manifests as romantic and financial opportunities that feel abundant rather than scarce. On Jupiter lines, this manifests as expansion that feels pleasurable rather than overwhelming. The combination of grace and growth is almost magical in its ease.

Mars-Saturn Harmonious Aspects

Mars trine Saturn or Mars sextile Saturn combines drive with discipline, action with structure, courage with caution. This creates sustained productive effort rather than scattered energy or paralyzed inaction. On Mars lines, this manifests as entrepreneurial ventures that have staying power, athletic training that builds genuine skill, or assertiveness that's respected rather than resisted. On Saturn lines, this manifests as hard work that feels energizing rather than depleting.

Mercury-Uranus Harmonious Aspects

Mercury trine Uranus or Mercury sextile Uranus creates brilliance, innovation, and breakthrough thinking. Communication becomes original, quick, and insightful. On Mercury lines, this manifests as genius-level intellectual work, innovative problem-solving, and communication that surprises and enlightens. On Uranus lines, this manifests as revolutionary ideas that can be articulated clearly and implemented practically.

Moon-Neptune Harmonious Aspects

Moon trine Neptune or Moon sextile Neptune creates emotional intuition, spiritual sensitivity, and artistic imagination. Feeling and vision flow together naturally. On Moon lines, this manifests as emotional experiences that carry spiritual meaning, homes that feel sacred, and instincts that access deeper wisdom. On Neptune lines, this manifests as spiritual practices that feel emotionally safe and mystical experiences that integrate smoothly into daily life.

Sun-Jupiter Harmonious Aspects

Sun trine Jupiter or Sun sextile Jupiter creates natural confidence, optimistic outlook, and fortunate life circumstances. Identity expansion feels natural and opportunities align with authentic self-expression. On Sun lines, success comes through being yourself without compromise. On Jupiter lines, growth enhances rather than overshadows core identity. The shadow involves overconfidence or taking opportunities for granted.

Moon-Venus Harmonious Aspects

Moon trine Venus or Moon sextile Venus creates emotional grace, aesthetic sensitivity, and natural relationship ease. Emotional needs and desire for beauty align harmoniously. On Moon lines, home becomes aesthetically pleasing and emotionally nourishing. On Venus lines, relationships provide genuine emotional security. This aspect creates people who make others feel comfortable and valued effortlessly.

Mercury-Neptune Harmonious Aspects

Mercury trine Neptune or Mercury sextile Neptune creates poetic communication, spiritual understanding, and intuitive intelligence. Logic and mysticism integrate rather than conflict. On Mercury lines, writing and speaking carry spiritual depth and artistic beauty. On Neptune lines, spiritual insights can be articulated clearly and shared practically. Excellent for teaching mystical subjects or creating inspirational content.

Mars-Jupiter Harmonious Aspects

Mars trine Jupiter or Mars sextile Jupiter creates confident action, successful ventures, and fortunate timing. Drive and opportunity align naturally. On Mars lines, initiative leads to expansion and success. On Jupiter lines, growth feels energizing rather than overwhelming. This aspect produces people who take bold action and succeed more often than fail. The shadow involves recklessness disguised as confidence.

Venus-Saturn Harmonious Aspects

Venus trine Saturn or Venus sextile Saturn creates committed relationships, enduring beauty, and values that mature over time. Pleasure and discipline work together productively. On Venus lines, relationships develop depth and loyalty. On Saturn lines, hard work brings aesthetic rewards and relationship stability. This aspect produces people whose taste improves with age and whose partnerships deepen rather than fade.

Sun-Mars Harmonious Aspects

Sun trine Mars or Sun sextile Mars creates natural courage, physical vitality, and authentic assertiveness. Identity and action align without internal conflict. On Sun lines, you assert yourself confidently in alignment with core values. On Mars lines, action expresses authentic self rather than reactive impulse. This aspect produces people who know what they want and pursue it directly without apology.

Harmonious Aspects in Mixed Configurations

Real charts rarely contain only harmonious aspects. Most people have planets that simultaneously trine some planets and square others. Understanding how harmonious aspects function within mixed configurations reveals sophisticated strategic possibilities.

Example: Sarah's Mixed Venus Pattern

Sarah has Venus at 18 degrees Libra trine Jupiter at 19 degrees Gemini (harmonious) AND square Pluto at 20 degrees Capricorn (challenging). This creates a complex pattern where relationships bring both fortunate expansion and intense transformation.

On her Venus line in Paris, both aspects activated simultaneously. The Venus-Jupiter trine brought abundant romantic opportunities, social grace, and aesthetic pleasure. The Venus-Pluto square brought psychological depth, power struggles, and transformative relationships. Rather than one canceling the other, they created layered experiences.

The strategic insight: Sarah learned to use the Venus-Jupiter trine as resource for navigating Venus-Pluto intensity. The trine provided optimism and faith that helped her stay open during Pluto's transformative pressure. The square prevented the trine from becoming superficial ease. Together they created relationships that were both fortunate and transformative, expansive and deep.

This pattern repeats across all mixed configurations. Harmonious aspects don't eliminate challenging aspects—they provide resources for working with challenges consciously and successfully. When planning relocations, look for locations that activate both harmonious and challenging aspects when you're ready for supported growth rather than pure ease or overwhelming difficulty.

Transit Activation of Harmonious Natal Aspects

Transits to planets involved in harmonious natal aspects create powerful timing windows for activating those lines. When Jupiter transits your natal Venus that trines Neptune, the Venus-Neptune flow intensifies dramatically. Strategic timing multiplies the benefits of harmonious aspect activation.

Strategic Transit Timing

Plan short trips to harmoniously aspected lines during supportive transits to maximize ease and opportunity. When Jupiter trines your natal Sun that already trines Moon, you experience doubled trine energy—exceptional for recovery, celebration, or launching ventures from a foundation of natural advantage.

Use harmonious aspect lines during challenging transits elsewhere in your chart. If Saturn is squaring your natal Mars, being on your Venus line that trines Jupiter provides support and ease in relationships and resources while Mars works through necessary discipline and limitation. The harmonious line doesn't stop the challenging transit but provides balance and relief.

Example: Michael has Sun trine Saturn natally. During his Saturn return (Saturn conjunct natal Saturn), he relocated to his Sun line. The Sun-Saturn trine meant his identity development (Sun line) supported his maturation process (Saturn return) rather than conflicting with it. He established his business and adult identity through disciplined effort that felt aligned with authentic self rather than imposed from outside. The trine made the Saturn return productive rather than crushing.

When to Choose Lines with Harmonious Aspects

Lines involving harmonious natal aspects are your safe harbors, your recovery zones, and your places of natural advantage. Knowing when to choose these lines strategically can make the difference between burning out and thriving, between struggling unnecessarily and flowing with life's natural currents.

During Recovery Periods

After crisis, illness, major loss, or any period of intense challenge, choosing lines with harmonious aspects provides the ease and support necessary for genuine recovery. Your system needs rest, not more struggle. Your psyche needs flow, not more friction. Lines with trines especially create conditions where healing happens naturally rather than requiring constant effort.

When Building Something New

Starting new ventures, businesses, creative projects, or relationships benefits enormously from the support of harmonious aspects. You have enough challenges simply from the newness of what you're building. You don't need additional challenges from your location fighting against you. Harmonious aspects provide the foundation of ease that lets new structures develop without constant crisis.

During Major Transits Elsewhere

If you're experiencing challenging transits to other planets in your chart, being on a line with harmonious aspects to different planets creates balance and support. The harmonious line doesn't stop the difficult transit from doing its work, but it provides resources, ease, and flow in other areas of life that help you handle the challenging transit without becoming completely overwhelmed.

The Shadow of Ease: When Harmonious Aspects Become Obstacles

Harmonious aspects carry a subtle danger that practitioners often overlook: ease can prevent development. When everything flows naturally, you may never build the muscles that struggle creates. Understanding the shadow of harmonious aspects prevents wasted potential and complacency.

Common Shadow Patterns

Underachievement relative to talent: People with multiple harmonious aspects often possess remarkable natural abilities they never fully develop because there's no pressure forcing growth. They get good enough to succeed easily but never push through to excellence because they've never needed to struggle.

Taking advantages for granted: When opportunities arrive effortlessly, you may fail to appreciate or fully utilize them. The person with Venus trine Jupiter who always has money may never learn financial discipline or gratitude for abundance.

Failure to develop complementary skills: The person with Mercury trine Neptune may write beautifully but never learn practical organization. The person with Mars trine Sun may act confidently but never develop patience or reflection. Harmonious aspects can create one-dimensional excellence without well-rounded competence.

Strategic complacency: When life flows smoothly on harmonious aspect lines, you may avoid necessary challenges or growth opportunities that would serve long-term development. Comfort becomes an invisible prison preventing evolution.

Working Consciously with the Shadow

Intentionally add challenge: Set ambitious goals that require full development of harmonious aspect gifts. Use the ease as foundation for pursuing excellence rather than settling for adequacy.

Alternate between harmonious and challenging lines: Spend periods on harmonious aspect lines building strength and confidence, then move to challenging aspect lines for growth and development. Return to harmonious lines for integration and rest. This rhythm prevents both burnout and complacency.

Practice gratitude and consciousness: When experiencing ease from harmonious aspects, consciously acknowledge the advantage rather than taking it for granted. Use the flow as opportunity to support others, develop skills deliberately, or pursue meaningful challenges.

Professional Consultation Guidance

When working with clients who have significant harmonious aspects, your role includes both celebrating natural gifts and providing realistic assessment of shadow patterns. Many people with harmonious aspects don't understand why they underachieve or feel unfulfilled despite apparent advantages.

Key Guidance Principles

Help clients recognize harmonious aspects as opportunities requiring conscious development, not automatic success guarantees. Explain that natural talent without deliberate practice rarely reaches excellence. Point out specific ways they can build on harmonious aspect foundations rather than coasting.

Recommend harmonious aspect lines during appropriate timing. Clients recovering from trauma, launching new ventures, or navigating challenging transits benefit enormously from harmonious line support. However, clients seeking growth, character development, or breaking comfortable patterns may need challenging aspect activation instead.

Assess whether clients have ever experienced genuine challenge. Some people with multiple harmonious aspects have coasted through life without developing resilience or depth. For these clients, deliberately choosing challenging aspect lines for limited periods can catalyze crucial development that harmonious lines alone will never provide.

Track the interplay between harmonious and challenging aspects in complex charts. Most people have both. Show clients how to use harmonious aspects as resources for navigating challenges rather than as escape routes from necessary growth. The integration of ease and effort produces optimal results.

Understanding harmonious aspects in your natal web and knowing which lines activate them gives you powerful tools for strategic life planning. These are the locations to return to when you need renewal, the places to choose when you want ease, and the lines to activate when you're ready to build on natural advantages. However, true mastery requires also understanding when ease becomes limitation and when challenge serves growth better than comfort.

In the next chapter, we'll examine the opposite: challenging aspects and how they transform line experiences into growth opportunities that demand consciousness, effort, and courage. The integration of harmonious and challenging aspect understanding creates complete strategic capability for conscious geographic alignment.

Chapter Five

Challenging Aspects: Squares and Oppositions in Your Web

A client once told me she'd spent her entire life avoiding her Saturn square Mars. "I know it's supposed to be hard," she said. "So I've just... stayed away from anything that might activate it." She'd lived in comfortable locations, chosen safe careers, avoided risks. At forty-two, she was restless, unfulfilled, and wondering why life felt like she was watching it happen to someone else.

We looked at her chart together. I showed her that her Saturn square Mars wasn't a curse to avoid—it was a growth edge to engage consciously. The friction wasn't there to make her life difficult. It was there to make her strong, disciplined, capable of sustained effort toward meaningful goals. She'd been avoiding the very aspect that could have given her life structure and power.

This is what I've learned about challenging aspects over years of practice: squares and oppositions create friction, tension, and the irresistible pressure to grow. These aspects don't make lines bad or dangerous, but they do make them demanding. When you activate a line and that planet has squares or oppositions to other planets, you're not just experiencing that planetary energy. You're experiencing internal conflict, competing needs, and the requirement to integrate parts of yourself that don't naturally cooperate.

This chapter explores how to work with challenging aspects consciously rather than being blindsided by them. You'll learn when to embrace the growth they offer, when to avoid them for your own wellbeing, and how to prepare if you decide to activate lines with challenging natal aspects during difficult timing periods. Understanding challenging aspects transforms them from problems to avoid into opportunities to choose consciously.

How Squares Create Friction

Squares connect planets in different modes (cardinal, fixed, mutable) and incompatible elements. Fire squares water, creating steam and potential explosion. Earth squares air, creating stuckness versus restlessness. The planetary energies want different things, operate through different strategies, and don't naturally understand each other. This creates internal tension that can't be ignored.

When you activate a planetary line and that planet squares another planet in your chart, you experience this internal tension geographically amplified. The friction isn't imposed from outside. It's your own competing needs, desires, and drives made more obvious and intense by location. This can be growth-producing or overwhelming depending on your readiness and resources.

Rachel's Sun-Saturn Square on Sun Line

Rachel relocated to Denver on her Sun Ascendant line, hoping for increased confidence and visibility. Her natal Sun at 15 degrees Aries squared Saturn at 17 degrees Capricorn. Both cardinal signs creating a clash between spontaneous self-expression and cautious responsibility, between 'I am' and 'I should,' between shining and shrinking.

In Denver, the Sun-Saturn square became Rachel's daily reality in ways it hadn't been in other locations. Every attempt to express herself freely triggered internal criticism about whether she was being too much, too loud, too visible. Every effort to be responsible and appropriate felt like suppressing her authentic vitality. The square created constant internal negotiation between these competing drives.

The friction was exhausting but also revealing. Rachel began to see patterns she'd been unconscious of her entire life. She realized she'd been bouncing between extreme self-expression that felt reckless and extreme self-restraint that felt deadening. Denver on her Sun line with the Saturn square made this pattern so obvious she couldn't ignore it anymore. She was forced to find a middle path, integrating appropriate self-expression with appropriate responsibility rather than swinging between extremes.

After two years in Denver, Rachel had developed genuine maturity around self-expression. She could shine without being grandiose. She could be responsible without disappearing. The Sun-Saturn square hadn't become easy, but she'd learned to work with it consciously. The geographic amplification forced growth she might have avoided for decades in a more comfortable location.

Mode-Specific Square Dynamics

Not all squares create the same kind of friction. The modality (cardinal, fixed, mutable) fundamentally shapes how squares manifest and what integration strategies work best. Understanding mode-specific patterns allows precise prediction and targeted intervention.

Cardinal Squares (Aries, Cancer, Libra, Capricorn)

Cardinal squares create crisis through competing initiatives and action demands. You want to start multiple things simultaneously in different directions, creating scattered energy and burnout potential.

Cardinal square friction manifests as doing too much in conflicting ways rather than sustained, focused effort.

Mars in Aries square Moon in Cancer creates tension between aggressive independence and emotional security needs. On Mars lines, you push forward but feel emotionally unsafe. On Moon lines, you seek comfort but feel stagnant and frustrated. The integration requires initiating action that honors emotional needs rather than sacrificing one for the other.

Strategic approach: Cardinal square locations work for time-limited intensive projects where multiple competing initiatives serve a single larger goal. Build in mandatory rest periods and clear project endpoints. Without limits, cardinal squares create exhaustion through endless initiation.

Fixed Squares (Taurus, Leo, Scorpio, Aquarius)

Fixed squares create stubbornness, resistance to change, and power struggles. You dig in on both ends of the square, refusing to compromise or adapt. Fixed square friction manifests as being stuck between equally rigid positions, creating paralysis or explosive conflict when pressure builds.

Venus in Taurus square Pluto in Leo creates tension between security/comfort and transformative intensity. On Venus lines, you want stability but feel compelled toward depth that threatens comfort. On Pluto lines, you pursue transformation but resist releasing material security. The integration requires allowing transformation within stable structures rather than forcing total revolution or maintaining rigid stagnation.

Strategic approach: Fixed square locations require regular check-ins with trusted advisors who can identify when persistence has become destructive stubbornness. Build in flexibility practices (yoga, improvisational activities) that counteract fixed energy's rigidity. Avoid fixed square locations during periods requiring major life changes.

Mutable Squares (Gemini, Virgo, Sagittarius, Pisces)

Mutable squares create scattered energy, confusion, and difficulty committing to single directions. You adapt to everything, change constantly, and struggle with follow-through. Mutable square friction manifests as being pulled in multiple directions simultaneously without clear priorities or sustained focus.

Mercury in Gemini square Neptune in Pisces creates tension between logical analysis and intuitive knowing, between facts and faith. On Mercury lines, thinking becomes confused by mystical impulses. On Neptune lines, spiritual experiences lack intellectual grounding. The integration requires developing both rational clarity and intuitive openness without letting either dissolve the other.

Strategic approach: Mutable square locations require strong external structures and accountability systems. Schedule regular commitments, hire organizational support, establish non-negotiable routines. Without structure, mutable squares scatter into chronic incompletion and confused purposelessness.

Element Conflict Patterns in Squares

Beyond modality, elemental incompatibility creates specific friction patterns. Understanding how different elements clash reveals the exact nature of internal conflict and points toward integration strategies.

Fire-Water Squares

Fire wants action, passion, and immediate expression. Water wants feeling, depth, and emotional safety. Fire-water squares create explosive volatility or suppressed passion. You either act without feeling or feel without acting. Integration requires inspired action that honors emotional truth—moving forward while staying connected to authentic feeling.

Example: Sun in Leo square Moon in Scorpio creates tension between expressive visibility and protective privacy. On Sun lines, you shine but feel emotionally exposed. On Moon lines, you feel safe but invisible and frustrated. The work involves developing capacity to be visible while maintaining emotional boundaries, to express without oversharing.

Earth-Air Squares

Earth wants practical results and tangible progress. Air wants ideas, communication, and mental stimulation. Earth-air squares create tension between doing and thinking, between results and concepts. You either intellectualize without manifesting or work without vision. Integration requires grounded thinking that produces practical results—ideas implemented, communication that creates change.

Example: Venus in Taurus square Mercury in Aquarius creates tension between sensual simplicity and intellectual complexity. On Venus lines, you want simple pleasures but feel mentally restless. On Mercury lines, you have brilliant ideas but struggle to ground them physically. The work involves creating beauty through innovative thinking, manifesting concepts aesthetically.

Fire-Air Squares (Within Same Modality)

When squares occur between compatible elements (fire-air or earth-water), the friction is less elemental incompatibility and more modal clash. Fire-air squares create scattered enthusiasm—brilliant ideas generating action that lacks focus. The challenge is choosing direction rather than pursuing every exciting possibility.

Earth-Water Squares (Within Same Modality)

Earth-water squares create tension between practical security and emotional flow. You build structures that feel emotionally limiting or follow feelings that undermine practical stability. Integration requires sustainable forms that channel emotion productively—resources that support feeling, feelings that inform wise action.

The Growth Opportunity in Squares

Squares are often where the most significant personal development occurs because they create tension that can't be resolved by choosing one side and ignoring the other. You have to find ways to honor both planetary energies, to develop capacity for holding seemingly contradictory needs simultaneously, to mature beyond either-or thinking into both-and integration.

In astrocartography, activating lines with squares means you're signing up for accelerated growth work. The location won't let you avoid the tension. It will make the square more obvious, more pressing, more impossible to ignore. If you're ready for that work, it can be profoundly valuable. If you need ease or recovery, it will feel punishing.

How Oppositions Create Polarity

Oppositions place planets 180 degrees apart, directly across the zodiac from each other. This creates a seesaw effect, a tendency to project one end of the polarity onto others or onto external circumstances while identifying with the opposite end. Oppositions often manifest as patterns of attraction and conflict with people who embody the qualities you're not expressing yourself.

When you activate a planetary line and that planet opposes another planet, the polarity becomes especially activated. You might find yourself constantly encountering people or situations that represent the opposite end of your planetary axis. The challenge is recognizing that both ends belong to you and learning to express both appropriately rather than splitting them between self and other.

David's Venus-Mars Opposition on Venus Line

David moved to Barcelona on his Venus Descendant line seeking romantic partnership. His natal Venus at 12 degrees Libra opposed Mars at 14 degrees Aries. Venus in Libra wants harmony, diplomacy, accommodation. Mars in Aries wants direct action, assertion, conquest. The opposition created a split between receptive relating and active pursuing that David had never fully integrated.

In Barcelona, David found himself constantly attracted to highly assertive, sometimes aggressive partners. He would initially be drawn to their confidence and directness, qualities he struggled to express himself. But inevitably, conflicts would arise as his need for harmony clashed with their need for direct confrontation. He felt torn between accommodating them (Venus) and standing up for himself (Mars). The opposition played out in his relationships repeatedly.

After several similar relationship patterns, David began therapy and started working consciously with the Venus-Mars opposition. He realized he was projecting his own Mars energy onto partners, attracted to their assertiveness because he couldn't access his own. Simultaneously, partners were attracted to his Venus qualities but frustrated when he wouldn't engage in direct conflict. Both ends of the opposition were necessary. He needed to develop his own capacity for assertion without losing his diplomatic skills.

Barcelona became the location where David learned to be both Venusian and Martian, both receptive and active, both harmonious and direct. The Venus line activated the opposition intensely, but this intensity forced integration work that transformed his relationship patterns permanently. Had he been somewhere more comfortable, he might have avoided this essential developmental work.

Opposition Axis Integration Techniques

Oppositions require sophisticated integration work beyond simple awareness. These techniques help move from projection and splitting to genuine embodiment of both polarities.

Core Integration Practices

Conscious alternation: Deliberately practice expressing both ends of the opposition at different times or in different contexts. If you have Sun-Moon opposition, spend mornings in solar expression (action, visibility) and evenings in lunar expression (feeling, retreat). This builds capacity for both rather than identifying with one.

Projection recognition: When you feel strong attraction or repulsion to people, ask what quality they're expressing that you struggle to embody. The intensity often signals projection of your opposition's rejected pole. The work involves owning and developing that quality yourself rather than outsourcing it to others.

Third-point synthesis: Find activities or practices that require both poles simultaneously. Venus-Mars oppositions integrate through partner dancing (receptivity and assertion). Mercury-Jupiter oppositions integrate through teaching (detail and vision). The synthesis transcends either-or into both-and.

Example: Jennifer has Mercury in Virgo opposite Jupiter in Pisces. She struggled between analytical precision and visionary inspiration, between criticism and faith. On her Mercury line in Seattle, she began teaching meditation (Jupiter) using precise instructions (Mercury). The synthesis activity required both poles—mystical experience communicated clearly. Through teaching, she developed capacity to hold both simultaneously rather than switching between them.

Projection and Reclamation

Oppositions in astrocartography often manifest through projection mechanisms becoming especially obvious. You keep encountering external representations of the projected planet because the location makes the opposition more active. The gift is that projection becomes so obvious you're forced to recognize and reclaim it. The challenge is that this recognition requires genuine psychological work and willingness to own disowned parts of yourself.

Orb Considerations in Challenging Aspects

As with harmonious aspects, orb tightness significantly affects how challenging aspects manifest. Tight challenging aspects create consistent friction requiring constant work. Wide challenging aspects create sporadic difficulties that emerge under stress or during relevant transits.

Tight Orbs (0-3 degrees)

Exact or near-exact squares and oppositions create core personality challenges you work with constantly. These aspects define major life themes and growth edges. On relevant lines, the friction is immediately intense and unavoidable. Preparation and support become essential.

Example: Michael has Mars at 10 degrees Cancer square Saturn at 10 degrees Libra (exact 0-degree orb). This precise aspect creates constant tension between assertion and restraint, between action and caution. On any Mars or Saturn line, the square dominates experience powerfully. He can never escape this tension—it's fundamental to his psyche. The work involves conscious integration rather than resolution.

Wide Orbs (6-10 degrees)

Wider challenging aspects create conditional friction that surfaces during challenging times but may barely register during stable periods. These aspects provide growth edges that don't constantly dominate. They're easier to work with consciously because you have more control over when to engage them.

Example: Lisa has Venus at 15 degrees Gemini square Neptune at 23 degrees Pisces (8-degree orb). This wide square creates occasional confusion in relationships or idealization that leads to disappointment, but not constant romantic chaos. On her Venus line in Paris, the square activated strongly during Neptune transits or relationship stress, but remained quiet during stable periods. She learned to recognize early warning signs and engage therapeutic support preemptively.

Planetary Combinations: Common Challenging Aspects

Different challenging aspect combinations create different flavors of friction and different growth opportunities. Understanding specific planetary squares and oppositions helps you predict what kind of work each line will demand when activated.

Moon-Saturn Challenging Aspects

Moon square or opposite Saturn creates tension between emotional needs and responsible limits, between vulnerability and self-protection, between needing care and being self-sufficient. On Moon lines, this manifests as emotional restriction, difficulty accessing comfort, or excessive self-criticism around feelings. On Saturn lines, this manifests as work and responsibility feeling emotionally draining or isolating. The integration challenge is learning appropriate emotional boundaries without shutting down entirely.

Venus-Pluto Challenging Aspects

Venus square or opposite Pluto creates intensity, obsession, and power dynamics in relationships. Love becomes transformation, sometimes through crisis. On Venus lines, this manifests as passionate but potentially destructive relationships, jealousy, possessiveness, or profound intimacy that requires psychological depth work. On Pluto lines, this manifests as relationships that force shadow integration, power struggles around love and money, or transformative partnerships that completely remake your value system.

Mars-Neptune Challenging Aspects

Mars square or opposite Neptune creates confusion around action, scattered energy, or spiritual bypassing of necessary assertion. On Mars lines, this manifests as difficulty taking direct action, confusion about what you actually want, or energy that dissipates rather than accomplishing goals. On Neptune lines, this manifests as spiritual practices that avoid rather than enhance embodied action, or idealism that prevents practical steps. The integration challenge is learning inspired action that's both spiritually aligned and practically effective.

Mercury-Jupiter Challenging Aspects

Mercury square or opposite Jupiter can create overconfidence, scattered thinking, or promises bigger than practical follow-through. On Mercury lines, this manifests as brilliant ideas without sufficient detail work, communication that oversells, or learning that's broad but shallow. On Jupiter lines, this manifests as expansion without adequate planning, optimism without reality testing, or philosophy without grounded application. The integration challenge is combining vision with practical thinking.

Sun-Uranus Challenging Aspects

Sun square or opposite Uranus creates tension between authentic self-expression and rebellious uniqueness, between integration and alienation. On Sun lines, this manifests as sudden identity shifts, restlessness with conventional life paths, or brilliance that feels disconnected from community. On Uranus lines, this manifests as revolutionary impulses that struggle to maintain coherent identity, or innovation that lacks personal groundedness. The integration challenge is being both genuinely yourself and genuinely connected.

Sun-Pluto Challenging Aspects

Sun square or opposite Pluto creates intense power struggles around identity, compulsive self-transformation, or destructive ego patterns. On Sun lines, identity becomes battleground for control and transformation. On Pluto lines, personal power overwhelms authentic self-expression. The integration challenge involves developing genuine power without egotism, transforming without losing core self. Therapy essential for conscious work.

Moon-Uranus Challenging Aspects

Moon square or opposite Uranus creates emotional instability, sudden mood shifts, or rebellion against security needs. On Moon lines, home feels restrictive and you crave constant change. On Uranus lines, innovation creates emotional chaos and instability. The integration challenge involves honoring both emotional security and freedom, creating stable structures that allow change.

Mercury-Saturn Challenging Aspects

Mercury square or opposite Saturn creates mental self-criticism, communication blocks, or excessive caution in thinking. On Mercury lines, expression feels inhibited by fear of being wrong or inadequate. On Saturn lines, responsibilities overwhelm mental clarity or creative thinking. The integration challenge involves developing disciplined thinking without paralytic perfectionism.

Venus-Uranus Challenging Aspects

Venus square or opposite Uranus creates erratic relationship patterns, fear of commitment, or attraction to unavailable partners. On Venus lines, relationships feel suffocating or you sabotage intimacy through sudden changes. On Uranus lines, innovation disrupts relationship stability repeatedly. The integration challenge involves creating relationships that honor both connection and freedom.

Mars-Pluto Challenging Aspects

Mars square or opposite Pluto creates explosive rage, power struggles, or compulsive action. On Mars lines, assertion becomes destructive intensity or violent breakthrough. On Pluto lines, transformation demands forceful action that may overwhelm. The integration challenge involves wielding power responsibly, transforming through conscious will rather than compulsive force. Anger management and shadow work essential.

Sun-Neptune Challenging Aspects

Sun square or opposite Neptune creates identity confusion, spiritual bypassing, or martyrdom patterns. On Sun lines, ego dissolves into confusion about who you actually are. On Neptune lines, spiritual pursuits undermine practical identity development. The integration challenge involves developing both spiritual openness and strong boundaries, mysticism grounded in authentic self.

When to AVOID Lines with Challenging Aspects

Knowing when NOT to activate challenging aspect lines is as important as knowing when to embrace them. These aspects can create genuine crisis, breakdown, and overwhelm when timing or resources are inadequate. Professional astrocartographers must assess client readiness honestly rather than encouraging growth work that could cause harm.

Avoid Challenging Aspect Lines When

- You're in active crisis or multiple life areas are unstable
- Mental health is compromised (depression, anxiety, trauma)
- Physical health requires recovery rather than challenge
- Support systems are weak or nonexistent
- Financial resources are inadequate for therapy/support
- Multiple difficult transits are activating the challenging aspects simultaneously
- You're already at capacity with other growth work
- You need rest, recovery, or gentle integration
- Recent major loss or trauma requires stabilization first
- Relationships are fragile and additional stress could destroy them

These aren't suggestions—they're essential safety parameters. Activating challenging aspects during vulnerable periods creates unnecessary suffering and potential breakdown. Sometimes the most advanced astrocartography move is choosing ease over growth.

Failed Relocations: Cautionary Tales

Not all challenging aspect activations produce growth. Sometimes they produce breakdown, crisis, or trauma. These failures teach essential lessons about timing, readiness, and the importance of adequate support.

Case Study: Robert's Mars-Saturn Square Breakdown

Robert had Mars at 8 degrees Aries square Saturn at 10 degrees Capricorn. Despite being in active recovery from depression and having minimal savings, he relocated to his Mars Midheaven line in New York hoping career pressure would force him into action. The Mars-Saturn square activated intensely—career demands (Mars MC) met rigid limitations and crushing self-criticism (Saturn square).

Within six months, Robert experienced complete breakdown. The relentless pressure to perform (Mars) combined with internal criticism and external obstacles (Saturn) created paralysis rather than productivity. He couldn't sleep, developed panic attacks, and burned through his savings without establishing career traction. He had to move home with family, requiring two years to stabilize.

The lesson: Mars-Saturn squares on Mars lines demand extraordinary resilience and support. Robert activated this challenging aspect while already vulnerable, without adequate resources, during multiple difficult transits. The timing was catastrophically wrong. Had he waited for stability, therapy, and supportive transits, the same location might have catalyzed growth rather than breakdown.

Case Study: Emma's Venus-Pluto Square Relationship Trauma

Emma had Venus at 15 degrees Libra square Pluto at 17 degrees Cancer. Fresh from divorce and emotionally raw, she relocated to her Venus Descendant line in Los Angeles hoping to find healing through new relationships. The Venus-Pluto square activated through intense, obsessive attractions that recreated her divorce patterns with amplified intensity.

Without therapeutic support or awareness of her Venus-Pluto patterns, Emma entered a destructive relationship characterized by jealousy, control, and emotional manipulation. The relationship ended traumatically after 18 months, leaving her more wounded than the divorce had. She required extensive therapy to recover from both relationships and understand how her Venus-Pluto square had manifested geographically.

The lesson: Venus-Pluto challenging aspects on Venus lines can create transformative relationships or traumatic ones. The difference is consciousness, therapeutic support, and readiness for shadow work. Emma wasn't ready. She needed healing first, then conscious relationship work on the Venus line with Pluto square awareness and professional support.

Recovery Strategies After Challenging Aspect Overwhelm

If you've activated challenging aspects at the wrong time and experienced breakdown or crisis, specific recovery strategies help restore stability and integrate the experience as learning rather than trauma.

Essential Recovery Steps

•Relocate to harmonious aspect lines: Move to locations activating your natal trines or sextiles. The ease provides recuperation space and resources for healing. Stay on harmonious lines until genuine stability returns—typically 6-18 months depending on severity.

•Engage professional support immediately: Therapy, medical care, or other professional support becomes non-negotiable. The overwhelm may have triggered underlying issues requiring expert intervention. Don't try to heal challenging aspect crisis alone.

•Practice self-compassion rather than self-blame: Overwhelming activations don't mean you failed. They mean timing or support was inadequate. The lesson involves better assessment, not harsh self-judgment. Learn from the experience without adding trauma through self-criticism.

•Map what happened astrologically: Understanding which aspects activated, which transits intensified them, and what support was missing creates wisdom for future decisions. This analysis helps prevent repetition while honoring the experience's teachings.

•Build resources before trying again: If you eventually want to work with that challenging aspect consciously, spend time building financial resources, support networks, therapeutic relationships, and inner resilience first. Success with challenging aspects requires preparation.

Working with Multiple Simultaneous Challenging Aspects

Some charts contain planets involved in multiple challenging aspects simultaneously. Sun square Saturn AND square Uranus creates double pressure on Sun lines. Venus opposite Mars AND square Pluto creates triple relationship intensity on Venus lines. Understanding cumulative effects prevents overwhelming activation.

Cumulative Effect Principles

Each additional challenging aspect multiplies difficulty rather than simply adding to it. One square creates focused growth work. Three squares to the same planet create potential overwhelm requiring exceptional consciousness and support. Assess readiness realistically.

Example: Patricia has Moon at 12 degrees Gemini square Saturn at 14 degrees Virgo, square Neptune at 15 degrees Pisces, and opposite

Pluto at 13 degrees Sagittarius. Her Moon participates in FOUR challenging aspects simultaneously. Any Moon line activation triggers this entire complex.

On her Moon IC line in Portland, Patricia experienced: emotional restriction (Saturn square), boundary dissolution (Neptune square), power struggles around vulnerability (Pluto opposition), and scattered emotional focus (mutable T-square). This wasn't one growth edge—it was four simultaneous intensive processes.

Patricia succeeded because she prepared extensively. She established therapy, built strong friendships, saved financial cushion, and chose Portland during supportive Jupiter transits. Even with preparation, the experience was intensely challenging. Without it, she would have experienced breakdown.

Strategic principle: For planets involved in multiple challenging aspects, either avoid their lines during vulnerable periods or prepare extraordinarily well. Never casually activate complex challenging aspect patterns. The potential for overwhelm is real and serious.

When to Embrace Challenging Aspects

Lines with challenging aspects aren't always to be avoided. Sometimes they're exactly what you need for the growth you're ready to embrace. Knowing when to deliberately choose friction rather than ease is an advanced astrocartography skill that separates strategic practitioners from those simply seeking comfort.

When You're Ready for Major Growth

If you've reached a developmental threshold where the old way isn't working anymore and you're genuinely ready to transform, activating lines with challenging aspects provides the pressure necessary to actually change rather than just contemplating change. Comfortable locations let you maintain patterns. Challenging lines force you to evolve.

When You Have Adequate Support

Challenging aspects become workable rather than overwhelming when you have strong support systems, therapeutic resources, spiritual practices, or community connection. If you're isolated and under-resourced, challenging aspects can be too much. If you're well-supported, they become growth edges rather than breaking points.

When Transit Timing Supports the Work

Sometimes challenging natal aspects combine with supportive transits to create optimal growth conditions. If you have natal Sun square Saturn but Jupiter is currently trining both your Sun and Saturn, the Jupiter transit provides the optimism and expansion that makes working with the square feel possible rather than crushing. Timing matters enormously with challenging aspects.

Professional Consultation Guidance for Challenging Aspects

Working with challenging aspects requires sophisticated assessment and ethical awareness. Whether you're evaluating your own readiness or guiding others, you must balance the genuine potential for growth with realistic acknowledgment of risk. This is where astrocartography becomes serious practice rather than entertainment.

The first skill is distinguishing actual readiness from stated readiness. Many people say they're prepared for growth work when they're actually seeking escape from current challenges. True readiness includes strong support systems, adequate financial resources, access to therapy or counseling, and relative stability in other life areas. If someone is already overwhelmed, adding challenging aspect activation often creates crisis rather than transformation.

Understanding the difference between growth and trauma is essential. Challenging aspects can catalyze development or create breakdown, and several factors determine which occurs. Current stress levels, available support, financial stability, therapeutic resources, and transit timing all influence whether challenging activation leads to empowerment or overwhelm. Your assessment should be realistic rather than optimistic. The goal isn't to be encouraging—it's to be accurate.

For any challenging aspect line consideration, establishing therapeutic support first is crucial. This becomes non-negotiable for squares involving Pluto, Saturn to personal planets, or multiple simultaneous challenging aspects. The support should be in place before relocation, not something to seek after difficulties arise.

Transit timing requires meticulous attention. Calculate all major transits for the year surrounding potential relocation. If multiple challenging transits will activate the natal challenging aspects during that period, postponement or alternative lines become necessary. Timing can make the difference between productive growth and genuine crisis.

Having exit strategies reduces anxiety and provides practical safety. Before activating challenging aspect lines, consider how you'll recognize if the intensity becomes too much and what you'll do if overwhelm occurs. Identify harmonious aspect lines that could serve as recovery locations if needed. This isn't pessimism—it's responsible planning.

The key is consciousness. Choose challenging aspects deliberately when you're genuinely ready for growth, adequately supported, and timing is favorable. Avoid them when you need recovery, lack support systems, or multiple difficult factors are already operating. Challenging aspects aren't obstacles to transcend—they're growth edges to engage consciously and strategically.

In the next chapter, we'll examine conjunction aspects, which blend planetary energies in ways that can be either harmonious or challenging depending on the planets involved and how consciously they're integrated.

Chapter Six

Mixed Aspect Patterns: When Harmonious and Challenging Aspects Combine

"I'm so confused," a client told me. "My Venus has a trine to Jupiter, which sounds amazing. But it also has a square to Saturn and an opposition to Uranus. So is my Venus line good or bad?" She laughed nervously. "I feel like I'm getting mixed messages from my own chart."

This is the reality of most natal charts. Most planets don't have purely harmonious or purely challenging aspects. They have mixed patterns—some trines and squares together, some sextiles and oppositions combined. These mixed patterns create complexity that requires nuanced understanding.

This chapter teaches you how to evaluate which aspects dominate when multiple aspect types operate simultaneously. You'll learn a systematic weighting system that transforms confusing mixed patterns into clear strategic guidance. By the end, you'll be able to look at a complex aspect web and confidently assess what the actual experience will be on that line.

Reading Complex Webs

When a planet has both harmonious and challenging aspects, your line experience will reflect both, but not equally. Tight-orb aspects dominate over wide-orb aspects. Personal planet aspects feel more immediate than outer planet aspects. Multiple harmonious aspects can soften a single challenging aspect. Multiple challenging aspects can overwhelm a single harmonious aspect.

The Aspect Weighting System: Calculating Dominance

Professional astrocartography requires systematic assessment of which aspects dominate mixed patterns. This weighting system provides practical methodology for evaluating relative strength when planets have multiple aspects simultaneously.

Primary Weighting Factors

1. ORB TIGHTNESS (Most important factor):

0-1 degree = Weight of 8 points

2-3 degrees = Weight of 6 points

4-5 degrees = Weight of 4 points

6-7 degrees = Weight of 2 points

8-10 degrees = Weight of 1 point

2. ASPECT TYPE:

Conjunction = Weight of 8 points (fusion is strongest)

Opposition = Weight of 6 points (polarity very active)

Square = Weight of 6 points (friction very active)

Trine = Weight of 4 points (ease is reliable)

Sextile = Weight of 2 points (opportunity requires activation)

3. PLANET TYPE:

Personal planets (Sun, Moon, Mercury, Venus, Mars) = Weight of 4 points

Social planets (Jupiter, Saturn) = Weight of 2 points

Outer planets (Uranus, Neptune, Pluto) = Weight of 1 point

4. CONFIGURATION INVOLVEMENT:

Part of T-Square, Grand Trine, or Grand Cross = Add 2 points

Stellium involvement = Add 2 points

Isolated aspect = No additional points

Calculation Method

For each aspect a planet makes, add: Orb points + Aspect Type points + Planet Type points + Configuration points = Total Weight

Then compare total weights: Harmonious aspects total vs Challenging aspects total. Whichever has higher total weight dominates the pattern. If totals within 20% of each other = Balanced mixed pattern.

Jennifer's Complex Venus Example

Jennifer has Venus at 18 degrees Libra with four aspects: trine to Jupiter (2-degree orb), square to Saturn (3-degree orb), sextile to Mars (1-degree orb), and opposition to Uranus (1-degree orb). All tight orbs create balanced complexity.

WEIGHTING ANALYSIS:

Harmonious Aspects:

Venus trine Jupiter (2° orb): 6 (orb) + 4 (trine) + 2 (Jupiter) + 0 (isolated) = 12 points

Venus sextile Mars (1° orb): 8 (orb) + 2 (sextile) + 4 (Mars) + 0 (isolated) = 14 points

Harmonious Total: 26 points

Challenging Aspects:

Venus square Saturn (3° orb): 6 (orb) + 6 (square) + 2 (Saturn) + 0 (isolated) = 14 points

Venus opposition Uranus (1° orb): 8 (orb) + 6 (opposition) + 1 (Uranus) + 0 (isolated) = 15 points

Challenging Total: 29 points

Interpretation:

Harmonious total = 26 points, Challenging total = 29 points. Challenging aspects slightly dominate but pattern is essentially balanced. Venus lines require navigation of all four dynamics simultaneously.

When Harmonious Aspects Dominate

Marcus has Moon at 10 degrees Cancer with tight trines to Venus and Neptune (Grand Trine in Water), plus wide square to Mars. Harmonious total = 46 points, Challenging = 10 points. Over 4:1 ratio means Moon lines will be predominantly easy with occasional manageable friction.

When Challenging Aspects Dominate

Robert has Saturn in T-Square with tight squares to Sun and Moon, plus trine to Neptune. Challenging total = 40 points, Harmonious = 5 points. Over 4:1 ratio means Saturn lines will be intensely demanding with occasional spiritual relief.

Integration Practices for Mixed Patterns

Daily aspect tracking: Note which aspects activate most strongly each day. Pattern recognition reveals when different aspects emerge, allowing conscious choice rather than unconscious reactivity.

Aspect-specific practices: Develop weekly rhythms honoring all aspects. Monday-Tuesday = one aspect focus, Wednesday-Thursday = another. This prevents any single aspect from dominating unconsciously.

Professional Assessment Protocol

Five-step protocol: (1) Map all aspects, (2) Apply weighting system, (3) Identify configurations, (4) Analyze element/mode distribution, (5) Map upcoming transits. Systematic assessment prevents oversimplification.

When to Simplify vs Embrace Complexity

Choose simpler lines during crisis, recovery, or when building foundations. Choose complex mixed patterns when ready for sophisticated development, well-supported, and during supportive transits. Strategic choice based on readiness, not random.

CONCLUSION: Mixed aspect patterns require nuanced understanding and conscious navigation. The weighting system provides practical methodology. Integration practices offer concrete tools. Success depends on preparation, consciousness, and strategic timing rather than hoping complexity resolves itself.

Chapter Seven

Special Points at Professional Depth

In Discover, you learned the foundational special points: the Lunar Nodes, Chiron, Juno, the Vertex, Part of Fortune, and Black Moon Lilith. You understand what they represent and how their lines function geographically. That knowledge serves as your foundation. Now we go deeper.

Professional astrocartography interpretation requires more than basic keyword meanings. You need to understand how these points evolve over time, how they interact with planetary lines and each other, and when specific points become critical in a client's chart. You need to recognize which points matter most for which life questions, and how to layer complex information without overwhelming the people you serve.

This chapter advances your understanding in two directions. First, we deepen your work with the special points you already know, moving from basic interpretation to professional mastery. Second, we expand your toolkit by introducing additional asteroids and Arabic lots that add sophisticated nuance to location analysis.

The key to professional-level work isn't using every possible point in every chart. It's knowing which points to emphasize when, and how to weave complex astrological signatures into clear, useful guidance. That discernment comes through practice, but it begins with deeper knowledge of what each point offers at the mastery level.

Part One: Deepening the Foundation

The special points introduced in Discover become exponentially more powerful when you understand their advanced applications. Each point contains layers of meaning that emerge through professional practice. What follows represents the next level of interpretation for each foundational point.

The Lunar Nodes: Beyond Comfort and Growth

The basic interpretation of nodal lines serves most clients well. South Node locations offer comfort and ease. North Node locations demand growth and challenge. That framework remains accurate, but professional work requires understanding nodal dynamics that textbooks rarely address.

Nodal Returns and Geographic Activation

The Lunar Nodes complete a full cycle through the zodiac approximately every 18.6 years. This means you experience a nodal return, when the transiting nodes return to their natal positions, roughly at ages 18, 37, 56, and 74. These periods mark profound evolutionary crossroads, moments when the soul's journey demands attention and reorientation.

Nodal return periods intensify the significance of nodal lines. A person living on their South Node line during a nodal return may experience the stagnation danger acutely. The comfort that once felt supportive becomes suffocating. Conversely, someone on their North Node line during a nodal return often experiences breakthrough growth, as if the universe conspires to accelerate their evolution.

Pay attention to clients approaching nodal returns. If they're on nodal lines during these periods, the location's influence magnifies dramatically. These become powerful windows for intentional relocation, either moving toward North Node growth or consciously choosing South Node rest before the next growth cycle.

The Nodal Axis as Karmic Storyline

Amateur astrologers often treat the nodes as separate points. Professional interpretation recognizes them as an axis, a polarity that tells a complete story. The South Node reveals not just comfort but specifically what you've mastered in other lifetimes, skills and approaches you brought into this incarnation already developed. The North Node shows not just growth but precisely what your soul chose to develop this time around.

This karmic perspective transforms location work. South Node lines aren't merely easy; they're places where you unconsciously recreate familiar patterns, sometimes limiting ones. A client with South Node in Capricorn living on their South Node line might default to workaholism and emotional disconnection, recreating a pattern they've lived before. The ease isn't always healthy.

Similarly, North Node lines aren't just challenging; they're specifically designed to develop the qualities your soul needs to integrate. The discomfort serves evolutionary purpose. Your North Node in Cancer line won't just feel emotionally intense; it will specifically push you to develop emotional availability, nurturing capacity, and vulnerability if those qualities remain underdeveloped in your chart.

Nodal Lines Combined with Planetary Lines

The most powerful geographic locations often combine nodal activation with major planetary lines. When your North Node line crosses your Sun Midheaven line, for example, that location doesn't just offer professional visibility. It specifically calls you toward soul growth through public expression and leadership. The success that location offers comes through developing qualities that don't come naturally.

Conversely, South Node combined with challenging planetary lines presents complex dynamics. Your South Node with Saturn lines might feel comfortable precisely because you're familiar with restriction, limitation, and hard work. You know how to operate under those conditions. But that familiarity might keep you stuck in patterns of struggle you came to transcend.

When counseling clients about combined nodal and planetary lines, help them understand that easy and good aren't synonyms. Sometimes the most beneficial location feels uncomfortable because it's pushing necessary development. Sometimes the most comfortable location undermines growth because it lets you hide in what you already know.

Chiron: The Wounded Healer at Professional Depth

Chiron's basic interpretation as the wounded healer provides a starting point, but professional Chiron work requires understanding this asteroid's paradoxical nature. Chiron represents wounds that never fully heal, yet through engaging those wounds, we develop our greatest capacity to heal others. Geographic Chiron activation intensifies this dynamic in ways that demand sophisticated navigation.

Chiron as Teacher Archetype

While Chiron carries wounded healer associations, his mythological role was primarily as teacher. He educated heroes, passing wisdom gained through his own suffering to those who would become healers and leaders themselves. This teaching dimension transforms how we interpret Chiron lines.

Chiron lines aren't only about personal healing work. They're locations where you're positioned to teach what you've learned through your wounds. Many astrologers, therapists, coaches, and teachers discover they live on or near Chiron lines. The location doesn't just bring wounds to the surface; it creates conditions for transforming those wounds into medicine for others.

When clients resist Chiron line recommendations because they fear the pain, help them understand that Chiron activation on these lines differs from fresh wounding. The wounds Chiron represents already exist. The line simply brings them into conscious awareness where they can be engaged, processed, and ultimately offered as teaching. Avoiding Chiron lines doesn't heal the wound; it merely keeps it unconscious and therefore unusable as wisdom.

Transgenerational Wounds and Geographic Healing

Advanced Chiron work recognizes that many Chiron wounds aren't personally created but inherited through family lineage. Your Chiron placement often describes wounds passed down through generations, patterns of pain and limitation your ancestors carried and unconsciously transmitted. Geographic Chiron activation can bring these transgenerational wounds into focus for conscious healing.

A client with Chiron in the 4th house living on their Chiron line might encounter intense family-of-origin material, not because the location creates new problems but because it illuminates inherited patterns ready for transformation. The work they do in that location potentially heals not just their own wound but breaks cycles affecting their entire family system.

This perspective shifts how you counsel clients about difficult Chiron line experiences. When someone reports that living on their Chiron line brought buried family trauma to the surface, they're not being punished by the location. They're being given opportunity to address wounds that would otherwise pass to the next generation. The pain serves purpose beyond personal healing.

Chiron Crossings: The 50-Year Revelation

Chiron's orbital period is approximately 50 years, creating what astrologers call the Chiron return around age 50. This represents a critical life passage when the nature of your core wound and its potential as wisdom becomes fully apparent. Like nodal returns, Chiron returns intensify the significance of Chiron lines.

Clients approaching or experiencing their Chiron return while living on Chiron lines often report profound revelations about the purpose of their suffering. What felt like random pain or personal failure reveals itself as preparation for specific teaching or healing work. The wound transforms from liability into qualification.

Pay particular attention to clients in their late 40s through early 50s considering moves to or from Chiron lines. This period represents optimal timing for intentional Chiron work. They have enough life experience to understand their wounds deeply, yet enough vitality to transform that understanding into active service. Chiron lines during Chiron return periods can catalyze the shift from wounded to healer.

Black Moon Lilith: Shadow Integration and Authentic Power

Lilith work separates surface-level astrologers from those willing to engage the shadow. While popular astrology often romanticizes Lilith as wild feminine power, professional interpretation requires understanding that Lilith represents what we've rejected, suppressed, and exiled from consciousness. Geographic Lilith activation brings this rejected material back to demand integration.

True Lilith vs. Mean Lilith: Technical Precision

Professional astrologers must understand that Black Moon Lilith exists in two calculation methods: Mean Lilith and True Lilith. Mean Lilith smooths the Moon's elliptical orbit into an averaged position.

True Lilith uses the actual, oscillating apogee point. The difference between these positions can span several degrees.

Most astrology software defaults to Mean Lilith for consistency, but some astrologers prefer True Lilith for its precision. For astrocartography purposes, using the same Lilith calculation consistently matters more than which calculation you choose. If you generate a client's natal chart with Mean Lilith, use Mean Lilith for their astrocartography map. Mixing calculations creates confusion and undermines interpretation accuracy.

When clients report Lilith line experiences that don't match your interpretation, verify which Lilith calculation was used. Occasionally, an experience that seems off for Mean Lilith perfectly matches True Lilith, or vice versa. This technical detail matters for professional credibility.

Lilith in Professional and Creative Work

While Lilith carries strong associations with sexuality and relationships, her influence extends powerfully into professional and creative realms. Lilith represents refusal to be controlled, domesticated, or limited by social expectations. In career contexts, this energy manifests as entrepreneurial independence, creative rebellion against industry norms, and willingness to pursue unconventional paths.

Artists, writers, and creatives often thrive on Lilith lines because these locations support work that challenges taboos, addresses uncomfortable truths, or refuses commercial compromise. The same energy that makes Lilith lines difficult for conventional employment makes them excellent for creative work that benefits from an outsider perspective or willingness to disturb comfortable narratives.

Entrepreneurs and business owners on Lilith lines frequently report doing things their own way despite industry pressure to conform. They create businesses that reflect authentic values rather than market trends. They're willing to be controversial if authenticity requires it. The Lilith energy that resists external control becomes an asset when building something genuinely original.

Shadow Integration: When Lilith Becomes Destructive

The shadow side of Lilith involves reactive destruction rather than empowered authenticity. When clients don't consciously engage Lilith energy, it manifests as unnecessary conflict, self-sabotage disguised as independence, and burning bridges that could have remained intact. Professional Lilith work requires helping clients distinguish between healthy boundary-setting and destructive defensiveness.

On Lilith lines, clients may attract strong reactions from others. Some people find their authenticity magnetic and inspiring. Others feel threatened and respond with rejection or attack. The question isn't whether these reactions occur but how the client responds to them. Lilith at her highest remains fierce but not cruel, independent but not isolated, powerful but not destructive.

When counseling clients struggling with Lilith line experiences, investigate whether they're confusing authenticity with aggression. True Lilith power doesn't require making others wrong or small. It simply refuses to make itself wrong or small to accommodate others' discomfort. That distinction determines whether Lilith energy becomes liberating or limiting.

Juno: Partnership at the Mastery Level

Basic Juno interpretation focuses on romantic partnership and marriage, but professional understanding recognizes Juno's broader significance in any committed, equal relationship structure. Business partnerships, creative collaborations, and long-term professional alliances all fall under Juno's domain. Geographic Juno activation influences how partnerships form and function in specific locations.

Juno in Business and Professional Partnerships

While Venus attracts people and creates pleasant connections, Juno determines whether those connections evolve into committed, functional partnerships. In business contexts, this distinction matters enormously. You might enjoy networking on Venus lines (pleasure, attraction, ease), but serious business partnerships that require trust, commitment, and shared responsibility often form or function best on Juno lines.

Entrepreneurs and business owners on Juno lines frequently report that the location brings partners who want serious involvement rather than casual collaboration. These partnerships demand maturity, clear agreements, and willingness to navigate power dynamics. The relationships that form carry weight and consequence. They're not light or easy, but they can be profoundly productive when approached with commitment and integrity.

When advising clients about business locations, consider Juno lines if their work requires true partnership rather than solo operation. The challenges Juno brings around equality, fairness, and power serve beneficial purpose in professional contexts. They force necessary conversations about roles, responsibilities, and shared authority that casual collaborations often avoid until problems arise.

Power, Equality, and the Juno Initiation

Juno's mythological story involves power struggles with Jupiter. As Jupiter's wife, Juno held significant power yet constantly dealt with Jupiter's infidelities and the complex dynamics of being partnered to someone more publicly powerful. This myth reveals Juno's core themes: how do we maintain our power within partnership? How do we balance independence with commitment? What do we sacrifice for relationship, and what must never be sacrificed?

Juno lines often bring these questions into sharp focus. Clients on Juno lines may encounter relationships where power dynamics require constant negotiation. They might feel trapped between independence and commitment, struggle with being the less publicly visible partner, or face situations where partnership demands uncomfortable compromise.

These challenges aren't punishment. They're initiations. Juno lines teach what mature partnership actually requires, which differs dramatically from romantic fantasy or casual connection. Professional interpretation helps clients understand that Juno's difficulties serve developmental purpose. The goal isn't finding effortless partnership but developing capacity for committed relationship that honors both individuals' autonomy and the relationship's needs.

Part of Fortune: Advanced Timing and Annual Relocation

The Part of Fortune, introduced in Discover as a point of natural luck and flow, reveals additional layers when combined with timing techniques. Professional astrologers use Part of Fortune lines not just for general life planning but for specific annual intentions and temporary relocations that maximize opportunity.

Part of Fortune and Annual Profections

Annual profections, an ancient timing technique, move the angles of your chart forward one sign per year of life. When the profected Ascendant activates a particular house, that house's themes dominate the year. Combining this technique with Part of Fortune astrocartography creates powerful timing strategies for location work.

If your Part of Fortune occupies your 10th house and you enter a 10th house profection year, temporarily living on or traveling to Part of Fortune lines during that year maximizes professional opportunity. The profection activates career themes; the Part of Fortune line provides natural flow and luck within those themes. The combination creates optimal conditions for advancement.

This technique works for any house profection. Second house profection year? Consider Part of Fortune lines for financial opportunity. Seventh house profection year? Part of Fortune lines might bring fortunate partnerships. The technique isn't about permanent relocation but strategic temporary positioning during years when specific life areas receive profection activation.

Part of Fortune in Different House Systems

Part of Fortune calculation uses the positions of Sun, Moon, and Ascendant. Because the Ascendant position varies by house system (Placidus, Whole Sign, Equal House, etc.), Part of Fortune's position also varies. This creates potential confusion when clients consult multiple astrologers who use different house systems.

For professional consistency, choose one house system and use it consistently for all astrocartography work. Most modern astrologers use Placidus for astrocartography because it's widely available in software and allows comparison with other astrologers' work. Whole Sign houses are gaining popularity and work equally well if used consistently.

What matters isn't which house system is "correct" but that you maintain consistency within your practice and communicate clearly which system you're using. When clients bring charts calculated with different house systems, their Part of Fortune position may shift several degrees. Recalculate using your preferred system to ensure accurate line placement.

The Vertex: Fate, Free Will, and Surrender

The Vertex occupies unique territory in astrology as the point where fate and free will intersect. While most chart factors describe energies we can consciously work with, the Vertex represents experiences that feel beyond our control, encounters and events that seem destined. Geographic Vertex activation intensifies this quality in ways that challenge conventional notions of manifestation and intention.

Vertex Activations by Transit

While planetary lines represent relatively constant geographic influence, Vertex lines become particularly powerful during specific transit periods when outer planets aspect your natal Vertex. If transiting Saturn squares your natal Vertex while you're living on a Vertex line, that period often brings fated encounters with authority, limitation, or serious responsibility.

Similarly, Jupiter transits to natal Vertex on Vertex lines frequently coincide with fortunate "meant to be" opportunities. Uranus transits bring sudden, unexpected life changes that feel destined. Neptune transits create spiritually significant encounters or periods of divine confusion where normal logic doesn't apply.

For professional practice, track major transits to clients' natal Vertex when they're considering Vertex line locations. If they're approaching a major Vertex transit, temporary relocation to or travel along Vertex lines during that period can amplify fated experiences in potentially valuable ways. The intersection of Vertex transit and Vertex location creates particularly powerful moments of destiny activation.

Vertex in Relocated Charts

The Vertex position changes in relocated charts because it's calculated based on angles that shift with geographic location. This creates an interesting dynamic: your natal Vertex creates its own geographic lines, but when you relocate, you also acquire a new Vertex position for that location. Both points become relevant for interpretation.

Your natal Vertex line describes where fated encounters related to your natal chart themes occur. Your relocated Vertex describes what kinds of destiny-level events the new location itself activates. Advanced astrocartography work considers both: Are you on your natal Vertex line? Does your relocated Vertex create significant aspects to natal planets? How do these factors combine?

This layering can become complex quickly. For most clients, natal Vertex lines provide sufficient information. Reserve relocated Vertex analysis for clients doing deep location work, planning permanent international moves, or investigating why a location brought specific fated experiences despite not sitting on obvious lines.

The Paradox of Vertex Work: Control and Surrender

Vertex interpretation presents a philosophical challenge for manifestation-oriented astrologers. Most astrocartography work empowers clients to make conscious location choices based on desired outcomes. Vertex work requires different wisdom: recognizing when to surrender to experiences beyond your control rather than forcing specific results.

Clients living on Vertex lines often report that their normal manifestation practices don't work as expected. They set intentions, take action, and somehow life unfolds differently than planned. This isn't failure; it's Vertex activation. These lines bring what's meant to happen rather than what you think should happen. The skill isn't controlling outcomes but discerning which experiences to resist and which to allow.

Professional Vertex counseling requires helping clients hold both truth: they have agency in choosing whether to live on Vertex lines, but once there, they must surrender attachment to specific outcomes. They can prepare for significant encounters and life changes, but they can't control exactly what those will look like. This paradox of choosing destiny while releasing control over its specific form represents advanced spiritual work that not all clients are ready to undertake.

Part Two: Expanding the Toolkit

The special points covered in Discover provide foundational astrocartography interpretation. To work at mastery level, you'll want to expand your toolkit with additional asteroids that add sophisticated layers to location analysis. The four major asteroids—Ceres, Pallas, Vesta, and Juno—represent the largest and most astrologically significant asteroid bodies. We've already covered Juno extensively. Now we explore Ceres, Pallas, and Vesta.

Beyond these major bodies, certain smaller asteroids carry particular psychological and spiritual significance. Eros and Psyche, though smaller than the major four, represent archetypal soul dynamics that become powerfully relevant in specific client situations. Not every chart requires asteroid analysis, but when working with clients whose questions involve these themes, asteroid lines can provide breakthrough insight.

Ceres: The Great Mother

Ceres represents the largest asteroid in the main asteroid belt and carries profound significance in psychological astrology. Named for the Roman goddess of agriculture and grain (Greek Demeter), Ceres governs themes of nurturing, nourishment, mothering, and the grief that comes from loss and separation. Her mythological story of losing and regaining her daughter Persephone provides the template for understanding Ceres in astrocartography.

Ceres Lines: Where and How We Nurture

Ceres lines activate our capacity to give and receive nourishment. This manifests through food, certainly—many professional chefs, nutritionists, and those whose work involves feeding others live on or near Ceres lines. But Ceres nourishment extends beyond literal food to any activity that sustains life, provides care, or helps things grow.

On Ceres lines, you may feel called to nurturing roles: parenting, caregiving, teaching, counseling, or healing work that involves tending to others' basic needs. The location activates maternal instincts regardless of gender. You become more aware of what feeds you emotionally and physically, and what depletes you. Boundaries around caregiving become important themes.

The shadow side of Ceres involves giving too much until you're depleted, or conversely, withholding nourishment when hurt or angry. Ceres in her myth controlled the harvest and could bring famine when grieving her daughter's loss. On Ceres lines, watch for patterns of using food, care, or support as control mechanisms, or allowing others to drain your resources without reciprocity.

Ceres and the Geography of Grief

Ceres's mythological story centers on loss and reunion. Her daughter Persephone was abducted by Hades, leading to Ceres's devastating grief and the earth's subsequent barrenness. Though Persephone eventually returned (though only part-time), the story emphasizes that some losses never fully resolve. We learn to live with them rather than completely overcome them.

Ceres lines often become significant during periods of loss, separation, or grief. Clients report that living on Ceres lines during or after major losses—death of loved ones, divorce, children leaving home, miscarriage—brings the grief into full conscious experience. The location doesn't create the loss but provides geographic container for feeling it completely.

This can be therapeutic or overwhelming depending on the client's resources and support systems. Ceres lines during grief periods can facilitate deep healing by allowing full emotional expression. They can also feel isolating if the person lacks adequate support. When counseling clients about Ceres lines during loss, assess their capacity to process intense emotion and availability of supportive relationships.

Ceres Lines and Relationship with Body and Food

As goddess of grain and harvest, Ceres governs our most fundamental relationship with physical nourishment. Ceres lines often bring food, body image, and eating patterns into focus. This can manifest as healing (developing healthy relationship with food, recovering from eating disorders, learning to nourish yourself well) or as challenge (encountering food scarcity, struggling with body image, facing eating pattern disruptions).

Clients working on healing their relationship with food, body, and nourishment sometimes benefit from intentional Ceres line work. The location can support developing sustainable eating practices, learning to recognize true hunger versus emotional eating, and building capacity to receive nurturing from food without shame or control.

Conversely, clients with active eating disorders or severe body image struggles may find Ceres lines intensify these patterns without adequate therapeutic support. Like all astrocartography work, Ceres line recommendations require assessing whether the activation will serve healing or create overwhelm beyond the person's current capacity.

Pallas: The Strategist and Pattern Weaver

Pallas Athene, born fully formed from Zeus's head, represents wisdom, strategy, creative intelligence, and the ability to see patterns others miss. Unlike emotional or instinctual knowing, Pallas intelligence operates through logic, strategy, and skillful navigation of complex situations. Her geographic lines activate this particular form of intelligence and creative problem-solving capacity.

Pallas Lines: Strategic Thinking and Pattern Recognition

Pallas lines enhance your capacity to see patterns, devise strategies, and solve complex problems through creative intelligence. These locations benefit anyone whose work requires strategic thinking: business strategists, game designers, political advisors, therapists who work with systemic patterns, artists creating intricate works, or anyone navigating complex situations requiring sophisticated analysis.

On Pallas lines, you notice connections others miss. You see how seemingly separate elements relate within larger patterns. You develop strategies that work with existing structures rather than forcing solutions through willpower alone. The intelligence that emerges feels clear, almost crystalline, different from the intuitive knowing of Neptune or the emotional intelligence of the Moon.

Pallas energy works particularly well for creative problem-solving where conventional approaches have failed. If you're stuck on a project, problem, or life situation that requires new perspective, temporary time on Pallas lines can provide breakthrough insight. The location supports seeing old situations through fresh eyes and devising novel solutions to persistent challenges.

Pallas and Healing Through Wisdom

Pallas mythology includes her role as healer, though her healing differs from Chiron's wounded healer archetype. Pallas heals through wisdom, through helping people understand the patterns creating their suffering so they can change those patterns. Her healing is educational and empowering rather than nurturing or caretaking.

Therapists, counselors, and healers who work by helping clients see their patterns often have strong Pallas placements or live on Pallas lines. These locations support work that illuminates how systems—family systems, thought systems, behavioral patterns—create and maintain problems. The goal isn't sympathetic comfort but clear understanding leading to strategic change.

Pallas lines can feel less emotionally nurturing than Ceres or Moon lines while offering different benefits. They're excellent for periods when you need clarity more than comfort, when you're ready to understand patterns you've been repeating unconsciously, or when you want to develop strategic approaches to persistent life challenges.

Vesta: The Sacred Flame

Vesta, asteroid goddess of the hearth and sacred fire, represents devotion, focus, spiritual practice, and what we consider sacred. In ancient Rome, Vestal Virgins tended the eternal flame, maintaining their virginity not from fear of sexuality but from dedication to sacred purpose. This mythology reveals Vesta's core themes: commitment to what matters most, willingness to sacrifice lesser desires for greater purpose, and capacity for sustained focus.

Vesta Lines: Sacred Focus and Devotion

Vesta lines activate capacity for deep focus and devotion to what you consider sacred. These locations benefit anyone whose work requires sustained concentration, spiritual practice, or commitment to craft: writers, researchers, spiritual practitioners, artists developing mastery, anyone engaged in work that demands years of dedicated effort.

On Vesta lines, you naturally prioritize what matters most. Distractions lose their pull. You feel called to protect and tend your inner flame, whatever represents your deepest commitment or sacred purpose. The location supports discipline not through force but through clarity about what deserves your devotion and what doesn't.

The challenge of Vesta lines involves balance between dedication and isolation. Vestal Virgins served the sacred flame but lived apart from normal social life. On Vesta lines, you may feel called to withdraw from social obligations to protect time and energy for your work or practice. This serves purpose up to a point, but can become problematic if it creates permanent isolation or inability to engage with normal life demands.

Vesta and Sacred Sexuality

Vesta's association with virginity is often misunderstood as sexual repression. The Vestal Virgins' virginity represented self-possession rather than sexual denial—they belonged to themselves and their sacred purpose rather than to husbands or families. This distinction matters for interpreting Vesta's sexual themes.

Vesta lines can bring sexuality into focus as sacred practice rather than casual recreation. Some people on Vesta lines choose celibacy or periods of sexual abstinence to redirect sexual energy toward creative or spiritual work. Others develop tantric practices or approach sexuality as spiritual communion. The common thread is treating sexual energy as something precious requiring conscious direction rather than casual expression.

This doesn't mean Vesta lines mandate celibacy or make casual sexuality wrong. It means the location brings awareness of sexuality as powerful energy requiring conscious choice about how, when, and with whom to express it. Clients on Vesta lines often report naturally becoming more selective about sexual partners and more intentional about sexual expression.

Eros: The Passionate Pursuer

Eros, though smaller than the major four asteroids, carries potent archetypal significance as the god of desire, passion, and the creative force that brings things together. While Venus represents attraction and love, Eros represents the passionate impulse itself, the magnetic pull toward what we desire, the creative fire that drives pursuit of what we're passionate about.

Eros Lines: Following Passionate Desire

Eros lines activate your capacity to know what you truly desire and pursue it with passion. These locations work powerfully for creatives, entrepreneurs, and anyone whose work depends on maintaining passionate engagement. On Eros lines, you feel more alive, more connected to what genuinely excites you, more willing to pursue what you want rather than settling for what's merely acceptable.

The passion Eros activates isn't limited to sexuality, though sexual passion certainly intensifies on these lines. Eros represents any domain where you pursue what you desire with full engagement: creative projects that consume your attention, business ventures you're passionate about building, causes you're willing to fight for, experiences you crave having. The location helps you access and honor that passionate drive.

The challenge of Eros lines involves distinguishing between healthy desire and compulsive craving. Eros can manifest as life-affirming passion or as obsessive pursuit that ignores consequences. Professional interpretation helps clients harness Eros energy for creative and relational vitality without letting desire override wisdom or integrity.

Psyche: The Soul's Journey

Psyche's mythology involves transformation through impossible tasks and ultimate union with Eros, representing the soul's journey toward wholeness through trials that seem insurmountable. Her name literally means soul, and her astrological significance involves deep psychological work, soul development, and the integration of consciousness.

Psyche Lines: Deep Soul Work and Integration

Psyche lines create conditions for profound psychological and spiritual work. These locations attract therapists, depth psychologists, spiritual teachers, and anyone engaged in work that involves soul development. On Psyche lines, you're more likely to encounter experiences that push psychological and spiritual growth, that demand integration of shadow material, that require facing inner truth however uncomfortable.

The work Psyche lines demand isn't comfortable, but it serves soul evolution in ways surface changes cannot. These locations support people ready for transformational inner work, willing to question their fundamental assumptions about themselves, prepared to integrate rejected aspects of psyche into conscious awareness.

Like Chiron lines, Psyche lines work best when clients have adequate support systems and therapeutic resources. The location catalyzes deep work but doesn't provide the container for processing it. Recommend Psyche lines to clients who are actively engaged in therapy, spiritual practice, or other forms of supported inner work, and who consciously choose depth over comfort.

Part Three: Advanced Arabic Lots

Arabic Lots, also called Arabic Parts, represent an ancient astrological technique dating back to Hellenistic astrology. These calculated points combine positions of three chart factors to reveal specific life themes. The most well-known lot, the Part of Fortune, was covered in Discover. Professional astrocartography practice can incorporate additional lots for clients whose questions align with specific lot themes.

Hundreds of lots exist in traditional astrology, but most offer diminishing returns for astrocartography purposes. Three additional lots beyond Part of Fortune provide practical value for location work: the Lot of Spirit, the Lot of Eros, and the Lot of Marriage. These lots address questions clients commonly bring to astrocartography consultations and can provide breakthrough insight when skillfully applied.

The Lot of Spirit: Spiritual Purpose and Life Direction

The Lot of Spirit serves as daytime complement to the Part of Fortune. While Part of Fortune is calculated from Ascendant plus Moon minus Sun (or the reverse for night charts), the Lot of Spirit uses Ascendant plus Sun minus Moon (reversed for night births). These two lots form a pair: Part of Fortune describes where life provides natural flow and ease; Lot of Spirit describes where your conscious will and spiritual purpose find expression.

Lot of Spirit lines activate themes of purpose, conscious intention, and spiritual expression. On these lines, you feel called to live according to your deepest values and spiritual understanding. Work that serves higher purpose feels more compelling than work driven purely by material success. You're more likely to make choices based on integrity and meaning than convenience or profit.

These locations benefit people at life stages when they're questioning purpose and direction. Midlife career changes, spiritual awakenings, or periods of reorienting around values all benefit from Lot of Spirit line activation. The location doesn't provide easy answers but creates conditions where living purposefully becomes more important than living comfortably.

Lot of Spirit combined with Part of Fortune lines (when they cross or run nearby) creates powerful locations for integrating material success with spiritual purpose. These rare crossings suggest places where you can thrive materially while remaining aligned with soul-level values. Professional sports stars, actors, or business people who successfully integrate commercial success with spiritual integrity often have significant Lot of Spirit activations.

The Lot of Eros: Passionate Desire and Magnetic Attraction

The Lot of Eros, calculated from Ascendant plus Venus minus Spirit (or its reverse for night births), reveals where and what we're passionately drawn toward. This differs from Eros the asteroid, though both relate to desire and passion. The lot describes destiny-level attraction—what we're fated to desire, what calls to us with magnetic pull beyond conscious choice.

Lot of Eros lines intensify passion, desire, and magnetic attraction. These locations benefit creative work that requires passionate engagement, romantic relationships based on deep attraction, or any pursuit demanding sustained desire rather than mere willpower. On Lot of Eros lines, you feel pulled toward experiences and people rather than choosing them through rational decision.

The shadow side of Lot of Eros involves compulsive desire, obsessive attraction, or confusing passionate intensity with genuine compatibility. Like Eros the asteroid, the lot can manifest as life-affirming passion or as destructive obsession. Professional interpretation helps clients harness Lot of Eros energy for creative vitality and authentic desire while avoiding the trap of letting passion override wisdom.

Lot of Eros lines work particularly well for artists, creatives, and anyone whose work depends on maintaining passionate connection to their craft. The location doesn't make work easy but keeps the creative fire burning. Writers on Lot of Eros lines report that projects they might abandon elsewhere keep calling them back. The desire to create outweighs the difficulty of creating.

The Lot of Marriage: Partnership Destiny

The Lot of Marriage, calculated from Ascendant plus Descendant minus Venus (with variations by sect), describes destiny-level partnership themes. While Juno the asteroid shows what we need in committed partnership, the Lot of Marriage reveals where partnership itself becomes a destiny question, where we encounter the people we're meant to commit to, where relationship choices carry karmic weight.

Lot of Marriage lines bring encounters with potential life partners and situations where partnership decisions feel weighty with consequence. On these lines, casual dating tends to evolve quickly toward commitment or end clearly. You're less likely to maintain ambiguous situationships. Relationships that form feel significant, meant to be, carrying a quality of destiny or fate.

This doesn't guarantee happy partnerships. The lot describes where partnership becomes a central life theme, not where partnership necessarily succeeds easily. Some Lot of Marriage line experiences involve meeting significant partners; others involve learning crucial partnership lessons through challenging relationships. The common thread is that partnership itself becomes important soul work.

Combine Lot of Marriage line analysis with Juno lines for sophisticated partnership location work. Juno describes what kinds of partnerships you attract and what you need from them. Lot of Marriage describes where partnership becomes destiny-level significant. Locations where both lines activate suggest places where you meet people who both match your partnership needs and carry karmic significance in your life story.

Part Four: Professional Integration

The information presented in this chapter represents advanced astrocartography content that separates professional practitioners from enthusiastic amateurs. However, advanced knowledge becomes valuable only when skillfully applied. Knowing about twelve asteroids and five lots doesn't help clients if you overwhelm them with complexity. Professional mastery requires not just knowledge but discernment about when and how to apply that knowledge.

Layering Without Overwhelming

The greatest temptation for astrologers learning advanced techniques involves using everything they know in every chart. A client asks about relocation, and you present analysis involving ten planets, seven special points, five asteroids, and three lots. The client leaves confused and paralyzed by options rather than empowered to make clear decisions.

Professional practice requires selective application. Start every chart analysis with the ten major planets. These create the strongest, most reliable geographic effects. Once you understand the planetary picture clearly, ask yourself: does this client's question or situation call for additional points? If they're asking about marriage, check Juno and Lot of Marriage. If they're addressing grief, examine Ceres. If they're questioning life purpose, explore Lot of Spirit.

Use special points and asteroids to add nuance and depth to planetary analysis, not to replace it. A location on someone's Venus Descendant line becomes even more significant if it also activates their Juno line—you can explain that the location brings both romantic attraction (Venus) and serious partnership potential (Juno). But lead with the planetary information and layer the asteroid content as refinement.

The rule of thumb: if you mention more than three or four different points for a single location, you're probably overwhelming the client. Choose the most relevant factors and present those clearly. The goal isn't demonstrating how much you know but helping the client make empowered location decisions based on clear understanding.

Matching Points to Client Questions

Different special points and asteroids become relevant for different client questions. Professional discernment involves recognizing which points matter for which situations. Here's a practical guide to matching points with common client questions:

For relationship and partnership questions, prioritize Venus, Mars, Juno, and Lot of Marriage. For soul purpose and life direction questions, emphasize Lot of Spirit, North Node, and potentially Vertex. For healing and therapeutic work, focus on Chiron, Ceres, and Psyche. For creative passion and projects, examine Eros (both asteroid and lot), and potentially Pallas for strategic creative work.

For career and professional questions, Mars, Sun, Jupiter, and Saturn remain primary, but add Pallas for strategic roles, Vesta for work requiring devotion, or Lot of Spirit for purpose-driven career changes. For grief and loss situations, Ceres becomes central. For spiritual awakening periods, Lot of Spirit, Neptune, and potentially Vertex offer insight.

This matching process isn't rigid formula but practical guideline. The art of professional astrocartography involves listening carefully to what clients actually ask, understanding the deeper questions beneath their surface inquiry, and selecting the most relevant astrological factors for their specific situation. Sometimes a client asks about career but really needs partnership guidance. Sometimes they ask about relationships but truly seek purpose. Your job involves hearing what they need and providing appropriate astrological insight.

Case Study Approach to Integration

One effective way to demonstrate advanced point integration involves case study methodology. Rather than explaining every possible asteroid and lot to every client, present specific examples showing how these factors worked in real situations. "I had a client who moved to their Ceres line during a divorce, and the location provided exactly the nurturing they needed while processing grief about the marriage ending." Concrete examples make abstract astrological concepts tangible.

When you've identified relevant special points for a client's situation, explain one at a time with real-world examples of how that energy manifests. "You're asking about locations for serious relationship potential. In addition to Venus, I'm looking at Juno, the asteroid of committed partnership. I worked with someone who moved to their Juno line and met their spouse within six months. The location didn't make the relationship easy, but it brought someone ready for real commitment."

This approach accomplishes several goals: it educates clients about astrological factors beyond their basic knowledge, it demonstrates your expertise through concrete application, and it makes the astrological information feel practical rather than theoretical. Clients remember stories more readily than abstract principles. Case examples help them envision how astrological energies might manifest in their own lives.

Ethical Considerations with Advanced Points

Advanced astrological knowledge creates ethical responsibility. When you tell clients about Chiron lines bringing wounds to the surface, or Psyche lines demanding deep soul work, or Lilith lines activating rejected aspects of self, you're describing potentially destabilizing experiences. Ensure clients have adequate support systems before recommending challenging lines for intensive work.

Always assess client readiness for difficult astrological activations. Someone with active mental health challenges, recent trauma, or inadequate therapeutic support might benefit from easier planetary lines rather than intense Chiron or Psyche work. Your job isn't pushing clients toward maximum growth at all costs but helping them navigate location choices that serve their current capacity and resources.

Conversely, avoid underestimating what clients can handle. Some people specifically seek challenging locations for intensive personal work. They have therapists, support communities, and conscious commitment to transformation. For these clients, Chiron or Psyche lines might be exactly right. The skill involves discerning which clients need gentler options and which are prepared for deeper work.

Remember that you're not just providing astrological information but influencing major life decisions. Clients often relocate based on astrocartography consultations. Ensure your recommendations consider the whole person: their emotional capacity, financial resources, family situations, career demands, and support systems. Advanced astrological knowledge serves clients best when combined with practical wisdom about human limits and needs.

Moving Forward with Mastery

Mastering special points, asteroids, and lots represents ongoing practice rather than finished achievement. Each client consultation teaches you something new about how these energies manifest geographically. Each location experience you observe or personally undergo deepens your understanding of astrological principles in concrete application.

Continue expanding your knowledge. Research additional asteroids when clients present unusual questions. Experiment with less common lots when standard techniques don't fully address someone's situation. But always maintain your foundation in the major planetary lines. Advanced techniques enhance core astrocartography practice; they don't replace it.

The measure of professional mastery isn't how many techniques you know but how skillfully you apply the right technique at the right time for the right person. A master astrologer helping someone choose between two cities might reference only Sun and Moon lines if that's what the question requires. Another consultation might demand deep work with Chiron, Psyche, and Lot of Spirit. Discernment about when to keep things simple and when to go deep represents the highest level of professional skill.

Trust that your knowledge will be there when you need it. You don't have to use every advanced technique in every consultation to justify your expertise. Professional confidence allows you to meet each client exactly where they are, providing precisely what they need without overwhelming them with everything you know. That selective, skillful application of advanced knowledge in service of clear, useful guidance defines mastery in astrocartography practice.

Chapter Eight

Strategic Decision-Making: Integrating Aspects, Transits, and Timing

I knew within five minutes of meeting Jessica that she had a Scorpio stellium. The intensity was unmistakable—that penetrating gaze, the way she cut through superficial conversation straight to the depths, the palpable sense of power barely contained beneath the surface. When I pulled up her chart, there they were: Sun, Mercury, Venus, and Mars all clustered in Scorpio in her 8th house. She wasn't just Scorpionic. She was Scorpio on steroids.

Jessica came to me because she felt like she was drowning. 'I can't do small talk. I can't do shallow. Everyone says I'm too much, too intense, too deep. Should I try to be more... normal?' I looked at that four-planet Scorpio stellium and wanted to laugh. Normal? She could no more be normal than the ocean could be a puddle. Her concentration wasn't a bug to be fixed—it was her entire operating system.

We calculated relocated charts to see how her stellium moved through different houses. In New York, it fell in her 7th house—all that intensity focused on partnerships. Overwhelming. In Los Angeles, her 10th house—that power channeled into career and public life. Terrifying but potentially brilliant. She chose LA. Five years later, she's running a transformational therapy practice that only takes the most committed clients. Her 'too intense' became her professional superpower because she found where to direct it.

A stellium occurs when three or more planets cluster in the same sign or house, creating concentrated energy in a specific life area or archetypal theme. Unlike T-Squares and Grand Trines which involve three planets in geometric relationship, stelliums involve three or more planets gathered close together. When you activate any line involved in your stellium, you potentially activate all the planets in that cluster simultaneously, creating intense focus and power—or overwhelming concentration that dominates experience. This chapter explores how to work with stellium activation strategically.

You now understand natal aspects, transit activation, and major configurations. This chapter integrates everything into a practical decision-making framework. Whether you're choosing where to travel, where to relocate, or when to visit specific lines, this step-by-step process helps you evaluate options strategically rather than guessing or hoping for the best.

The Five-Step Decision Process

Every location decision follows the same basic structure. First, identify the planetary line or lines involved. Second, map the natal aspects for those planets. Third, check upcoming transits to those planets over the next two to three years. Fourth, evaluate whether transits will activate harmonious or challenging natal aspects. Fifth, decide based on the complete picture plus your current life circumstances and readiness.

Step One: Identify the Lines

Pull up your astrocartography map and locate the city or region you're considering. Which planetary lines run through or near that location? Remember that you're affected by lines within approximately 400 miles, with strongest effects within 100 miles. If multiple lines intersect at your chosen location, you'll be activating all involved planets simultaneously.

Example: You're considering Barcelona. Your map shows Venus Descendant line runs directly through the city, with Moon IC line about 200 miles away. Primary activation is Venus. Secondary weaker activation is Moon. Both matter, but Venus dominates.

Step Two: Map the Natal Aspects

For each planet involved, refer to your aspect web document created in Chapter 2. List every aspect that planet makes to other planets, noting aspect type and orb tightness. Pay particular attention to tight orbs (under 3 degrees) as these will manifest most obviously. Don't skip this step. The natal aspects are the hidden variable that determines your actual experience.

Example: Your Venus at 18 degrees Libra forms trine to Jupiter at 16 degrees Gemini (2-degree orb), square to Saturn at 20 degrees Capricorn (2-degree orb), sextile to Mars at 19 degrees Leo (1-degree orb). Three aspects total, mixed harmonious and challenging, all tight orbs. This means Barcelona will activate Venus, Jupiter, Saturn, and Mars simultaneously.

Step Three: Check Upcoming Transits

Use astrology software or online ephemeris to check what transits will cross your natal Venus (in this example) over the next two to three years. Focus on outer planets (Saturn, Uranus, Neptune, Pluto) which move slowly and create sustained activation. Note social planets (Jupiter, Saturn) which create year-long themes. Inner planets move too quickly to plan long-term relocations around them, but they matter for short trips.

Example: Checking your Venus at 18 degrees Libra, you see Saturn will be at 18 degrees Aries (opposing your Venus) in six months. Jupiter will trine your Venus from Gemini in eighteen months. Uranus is nowhere near your Venus degree for years. Two significant transits upcoming, one challenging and one harmonious.

Step Four: Evaluate Transit-Aspect Combinations

This is where everything comes together. When Saturn opposes your Venus in Barcelona, it will also activate your natal Venus-Jupiter trine, Venus-Saturn square, and Venus-Mars sextile. Saturn opposing Venus is already challenging. But your natal Venus squares Saturn, so Saturn's transit creates double Saturn pressure. However, your natal Venus trines Jupiter, which provides some optimism and ease. The Mars sextile offers energy if consciously activated.

The pattern that emerges: Barcelona during the Saturn opposition will be intense relationship work (Saturn opposite Venus) with double structural pressure (natal Venus-Saturn square activating), some fortunate opportunities (Venus-Jupiter trine continuing to flow), and available drive for conscious action (Venus-Mars sextile ready to engage).

When Jupiter trines your Venus eighteen months later, it activates your natal Venus-Jupiter trine (double harmony!), the Venus-Saturn square (but with Jupiter softening Saturn's restriction), and the Venus-Mars sextile (amplifying opportunity for action). This is excellent timing. Multiple layers of support.

Step Five: Make Your Decision

Consider the complete picture plus your personal readiness. Are you prepared for Saturn's challenges or do you need ease right now? Do you have adequate support systems for difficult transits? Are you excited by growth opportunities or depleted and needing recovery? There's no universally right answer. The decision depends on your current circumstances and what you're genuinely ready to handle.

In the Barcelona example, if you're ready for intensive relationship growth work and you have strong support, moving during the Saturn opposition could be profoundly transformative. Your natal aspects provide resources (Jupiter trine, Mars sextile) that make the challenge workable. But if you're already maxed out or need ease, waiting until the Jupiter trine period (eighteen months later) makes more sense. Same location, different timing, completely different experiences.

Decision Matrix Worksheet

Create a simple worksheet for each location you're considering. Location name and coordinates. Planetary lines involved with their angles (Ascendant, Midheaven, etc.). Natal aspects for each planet, listed by type and orb. Upcoming transits over next two to three years. Transit-aspect combinations (what does each transit activate in your natal web?). Overall assessment based on your current needs and readiness.

Fill this out completely before making decisions. The clarity that emerges from seeing the full pattern prevents surprises and helps you choose consciously rather than reactively. Keep these worksheets as you travel. They become valuable references for understanding your experiences and learning your personal patterns with different aspect-transit combinations.

Common Decision Scenarios
Scenario: Multiple Lines Crossing

When multiple lines cross at one location, you activate all involved planets simultaneously. Evaluate each planet's natal aspects, then look at how the planets relate to each other. If your Sun and Venus lines cross and Sun trines Venus natally, the crossing creates enhanced harmony. If Sun squares Venus natally, the crossing intensifies that tension. Crossings amplify whatever natal relationship exists between the planets involved.

Scenario: No Major Aspects to Line Planet

If the planet has no significant aspects, it operates more purely and independently. Your experience will be closer to traditional planetary line interpretation without modification from other planetary influences. This can feel clean and focused, or isolated and disconnected depending on the planet and your relationship to that energy. Unaspected Venus lines bring pure Venusian experience. Unaspected Saturn lines bring pure Saturnian experience.

Scenario: Conflicting Desires

Sometimes one part of you wants to go somewhere (career opportunity, relationship possibility) while another part hesitates. Check whether the hesitation aligns with challenging aspects in your natal web. If your Venus squares Saturn and you're hesitant about a Venus line despite wanting relationship, your Saturn square might be signaling that the timing or location will bring more restriction than ease. Trust the hesitation. It might be natal wisdom speaking.

Transit-by-Transit Guide

Understanding how transits activate your natal aspect webs transforms astrocartography from static map reading to dynamic strategic planning. When Jupiter transits your natal Sun, that transit simultaneously activates every planet that aspects your Sun—and when you're on lines connected to your Sun's aspect web, the activation intensifies geographically. This chapter provides planet-by-planet guidance for timing relocations and travels based on which transits are activating which aspect patterns.

Each transiting planet operates on its own timeline and carries distinct energy. Fast-moving planets (Moon, Mercury, Venus, Mars) create short-term activations lasting days to months. Slow-moving planets (Jupiter, Saturn, Uranus, Neptune, Pluto) create sustained activations lasting months to years. Strategic timing requires understanding both the transit's nature and your natal aspect web's structure.

Solar Transits: Annual Cycle of Identity and Purpose

The Sun completes its zodiac cycle annually, transiting each natal planet once per year. Solar transits activate identity, vitality, and life purpose themes. When the Sun transits a natal planet, it illuminates that planetary energy and every planet aspecting it.

Duration

The Sun spends approximately one month in each zodiac sign, creating month-long windows when specific natal planets receive solar activation. The exact transit (Sun conjunct, square, trine, or opposite natal planet) lasts 2-3 days with a 1-degree orb, though the surrounding weeks carry related energy.

Strategic Application

Plan short trips during solar transits to natal planets involved in important aspect webs. If your natal Mars trines Jupiter and squares Saturn, when the Sun transits Mars, travel to Mars line locations for 2-3 days of concentrated activation. Solar transits work well for testing lines before committing to longer stays. The activation is brief but clarifying—you experience the line's essential quality without sustained pressure.

Example: James has Venus trine Neptune and Venus square Pluto. Each year when the Sun transits his natal Venus (late Taurus), he experiences intensified romantic and creative themes. Traveling to his Venus line during this window amplifies the annual Venus activation geographically. The Sun illuminates both the trine's spiritual romance potential and the square's intensity. The 2-3 day trip provides concentrated insight into how his Venus web functions in that location.

Lunar Transits: Monthly Emotional Rhythm

The Moon completes its zodiac cycle in approximately 28 days, transiting each natal planet monthly. Lunar transits activate emotional responses, subconscious patterns, and immediate needs. Moon transits are the fastest, most frequent activations in astrology.

Duration

The Moon spends approximately 2.5 days in each sign, creating brief activations. The exact Moon-to-natal-planet aspect lasts hours, though emotional effects may linger for the full 2.5-day period while Moon transits that sign.

Strategic Application

Lunar transits work best for daily timing rather than relocation planning. However, lunar return charts (calculated when transiting Moon returns to natal Moon position monthly) reveal optimal short-trip timing. If you're planning a weekend visit to test a line, time it during supportive lunar transits to planets involved in that line's aspect web.

Track void-of-course Moon periods—when Moon makes its final aspect in a sign before changing signs. Avoid initiating important relocations or signing leases during void Moon. The lack of aspectual connection creates ungroundedness that manifests as forgotten details or unexpected complications.

Mercury Transits: Communication and Connection Cycles

Mercury completes its zodiac cycle in approximately one year, spending 2-3 weeks in each sign typically. Mercury retrograde periods (three times yearly for about three weeks each) extend stays in specific signs. Mercury transits activate communication, travel, contracts, and local environment themes.

Duration

Mercury typically transits each natal planet once yearly, though retrograde motion can create three passes (direct, retrograde, direct again) over several months. Exact Mercury-to-natal-planet aspects last 1-3 days depending on Mercury's speed.

Strategic Application

Mercury transits excel for short trips and location research. When Mercury transits natal planets connected to lines you're considering, visit for reconnaissance. The mental clarity and communication activation help you gather information and assess fit. Avoid signing leases or contracts during Mercury retrograde, especially on Mercury lines or when Mercury retrogrades over planets aspecting your Mercury.

Example: Rachel has Mercury trine Saturn and Mercury square Uranus. When transiting Mercury aspects her natal Mercury, she visits her Mercury line cities. During the trine activation, communication flows naturally and she gathers reliable information. The square activation brings unexpected insights but also technological glitches and communication mishaps. She avoids Mercury retrograde periods for serious Mercury line business.

Venus Transits: Love, Beauty, and Value Cycles

Venus completes its zodiac cycle in approximately one year, spending 3-5 weeks in each sign typically. Venus retrograde (every 18 months for about six weeks) extends stays and creates review periods. Venus transits activate relationship, pleasure, aesthetic, and financial themes.

Duration

Venus transits each natal planet once yearly in normal years, though retrograde can create extended activations or multiple passes. Exact Venus-to-natal-planet aspects last 2-4 days depending on Venus's speed.

Strategic Application

Venus transits provide optimal timing for relationship-focused travel and creative projects on Venus lines. When Venus transits natal planets aspecting your Venus, romantic and creative energy flows toward those planetary themes. Avoid beginning serious relationships or making major financial commitments during Venus retrograde, especially on Venus lines. Use retrograde periods for reassessing values and relationship patterns.

If your natal Venus squares Pluto, when transiting Venus aspects Venus or Pluto, intensity in relationships amplifies. On Venus lines during these transits, obsessive attraction patterns surface clearly. This awareness allows conscious choice rather than unconscious compulsion.

Mars Transits: Action, Assertion, and Energy Cycles

Mars completes its zodiac cycle in approximately two years, spending 6-7 weeks in each sign typically. Mars retrograde (every two years for 2-3 months) extends stays and redirects action. Mars transits activate drive, assertion, sexuality, and conflict themes.

Duration

Mars transits each natal planet roughly every two years. Retrograde motion can create three passes lasting several months. Exact Mars-to-natal-planet aspects last 3-5 days, though the surrounding weeks carry related energy due to Mars's relatively slow movement.

Chapter Nine

Aspects to Special Points: The Hidden Modifiers

I'll never forget the day my client Rebecca called me in tears from Edinburgh. 'You told me my Venus line would be amazing for love,' she said, voice shaking. 'But I just got my heart broken in the most devastating way possible.' I pulled up her chart, confused—her Venus line should have been supportive, flowing, easy. Then I saw it. Her Venus conjuncted her Vertex. That 'fated encounter' point I'd completely forgotten to mention.

Rebecca had experienced exactly what her chart promised—a relationship that felt destined, meant-to-be, significant beyond measure. What I'd failed to tell her was that Vertex encounters aren't always comfortable. They're evolutionary. Her Venus line brought love, yes. But her Venus-Vertex conjunction meant that love would arrive as a catalyst for soul-level transformation, not a fairy tale romance. Same line, same city, but understanding the Vertex activation would have changed everything about how she approached it.

That phone call taught me to never overlook the special points again. Beyond the ten traditional planets, your chart contains special points like the Lunar Nodes, Chiron, Part of Fortune, and Vertex

THE POWER OF PLACE: MASTER 115

that also form aspects to planets and create their own astrocartography lines. When planets aspect these special points, activating those planetary lines simultaneously triggers the special point's energy. This chapter explores how these often-overlooked aspects modify line experiences.

Understanding aspect activation transforms astrocartography from surface-level prediction to precise professional guidance. When you activate a Chiron line, you're not just activating Chiron—you're simultaneously activating every planet that aspects your natal Chiron, creating complex webs of experience that require sophisticated interpretation. This chapter provides comprehensive methodology for reading these multi-layered activations with professional precision.

Aspects to the Lunar Nodes

Planets aspecting your North Node or South Node carry evolutionary significance. The North Node represents growth direction, areas of development. The South Node represents comfort zones, familiar patterns. When a planet aspects either node, that planetary line becomes part of your soul's evolutionary journey in particularly focused ways.

Understanding the Nodal Axis Dynamic

The nodes form an axis—you cannot have an aspect to one node without creating a complementary aspect to the other. If Venus trines your North Node, it simultaneously sextiles your South Node. If Mars squares your North Node, it also squares your South Node. This creates polarity between evolutionary growth (North Node) and comfortable patterns (South Node) that plays out geographically.

Professional interpretation requires understanding both ends of the nodal axis simultaneously. Venus trine North Node and sextile South Node creates locations where relationships support growth (North Node trine) while maintaining some comfort and ease from past experience (South Node sextile). The aspect pattern tells the complete story.

North Node Aspect Patterns

Venus Trine North Node

If your Venus trines your North Node, your Venus lines support your evolutionary growth. Relationships, pleasure, and values align naturally with your soul's intended direction. On Venus lines, you develop the qualities your North Node represents through Venusian experiences. Love becomes a vehicle for evolution rather than a distraction from it.

Sun Conjunct North Node

Identity development IS your evolutionary path. Sun lines become powerfully aligned with soul purpose. These locations support stepping into leadership, visibility, and authentic self-expression in service of growth. The fusion of identity and destiny creates lines where being yourself advances evolution. Recommended for major life transitions requiring courage.

Mercury Square North Node

Mental patterns and communication styles conflict with growth direction. Mercury lines force releasing old ways of thinking and learning new perspectives. These locations challenge limiting beliefs and require intellectual flexibility. Excellent for education, therapy, or any work demanding mental evolution, but frustrating if you resist changing how you think and communicate.

Moon Trine North Node

Emotional development supports evolutionary direction naturally. Moon lines provide nurturing environments for growth. Home, family, and emotional security align with soul purpose. These locations feel safe while pushing development—rare combination of comfort and evolution. Ideal for building foundations while advancing spiritually.

Jupiter Conjunct North Node

Expansion and growth merge with evolutionary direction. Jupiter lines become doubly fortunate for development. Opportunities arrive that specifically serve soul evolution. Teachers, mentors, and philosophical growth support destiny. These locations accelerate growth through grace rather than struggle. Highly recommended for education, spiritual development, or career advancement aligned with purpose.

Saturn Square North Node

Responsibility and limitation create friction with growth direction. Saturn lines demand working hard for evolution—no shortcuts or easy paths. Structure serves development but feels restrictive. These locations teach that growth requires discipline, time, and sustained effort. Recommended only when ready for serious developmental work with patience and maturity.

South Node Aspect Patterns

Mars Square South Node

If your Mars squares your South Node, your Mars lines create friction with old patterns and comfortable behaviors. Action and assertion challenge what's familiar. This can be growth-producing or frustrating depending on your readiness to release South Node attachments. Mars lines demand you move beyond comfort zones rather than settling into them.

Venus Conjunct South Node

Relationships and pleasure patterns repeat familiar dynamics from past conditioning or past lives. Venus lines feel comfortable but may enable stagnation in love and values. You attract what you've known before—relationships that feel easy because they're repeating old patterns. Useful for rest and recovery, problematic if avoiding necessary relationship evolution.

Sun Opposition South Node (Conjunct North Node)

Identity expression directly opposes comfort zones. Sun lines force choosing between authentic self-expression and familiar safety. This tension catalyzes growth—you cannot be yourself AND stay comfortable. These locations demand courage to express who you're becoming rather than who you've been.

Jupiter Trine South Node

Expansion comes easily through familiar philosophical or spiritual patterns. Jupiter lines feel fortunate and comfortable, but watch for spiritual bypassing—using wisdom to avoid growth. These locations support rest through spiritual practice or teaching what you already know. Limit time here to prevent stagnation disguised as enlightenment.

Saturn Conjunct South Node

Limitation and responsibility feel familiar—you know how to operate under restriction. Saturn lines recreate patterns of struggle or discipline you've mastered before. This can provide stability through hard work, or trap you in unnecessary difficulty. Question whether Saturn's challenges serve growth or simply repeat known suffering.

Nodal Returns and Strategic Timing

The Lunar Nodes complete a full cycle approximately every 18.6 years, creating nodal returns at roughly ages 18-19, 37-38, 56, and 74-75. These periods mark profound evolutionary crossroads when soul direction demands attention and reorientation. Nodal line activation during nodal return periods intensifies significantly.

Strategic Nodal Return Relocation:

During nodal return years, South Node lines may feel suffocating rather than comfortable—the stagnation danger becomes acute. Conversely, North Node lines during returns often catalyze breakthrough growth, as if the universe conspires to accelerate evolution. Plan major relocations around nodal returns for maximum developmental impact.

If a client is approaching a nodal return (within 6 months before or after exact), assess their current location relative to nodal lines. Being on South Node lines during returns can trigger crisis of stagnation. Being on North Node lines can create breakthrough opportunities. Neutral locations allow internal processing without geographic amplification.

Aspects to Chiron

Chiron represents your core wound and your healing potential. Planets aspecting Chiron carry both wounding and healing possibilities. When you activate these planetary lines, you simultaneously activate your relationship to your wound, sometimes reopening it, sometimes healing it, often both.

Moon Conjunct Chiron

If your Moon conjoins Chiron, your Moon lines bring up emotional wounding and healing simultaneously. Home, family, and security themes carry both pain and medicine. These lines can feel tender, vulnerable, or profoundly healing depending on your stage of Chiron work. Expect emotional sensitivity and opportunities for deep emotional healing.

Sun Trine Chiron

If your Sun trines Chiron, your Sun lines create natural opportunities for healing through self-expression and identity development. Your core wound becomes integrated with your sense of purpose. These lines support healing work that feels aligned with who you are rather than separate from your identity.

Venus Square Chiron

Love wounds and self-worth challenges surface intensely on Venus lines. Relationships mirror unhealed patterns around deserving love, beauty, and pleasure. These locations demand honest examination of how wounds affect capacity for receiving love. Breakthrough comes through accepting imperfection while maintaining healthy standards. Therapeutic support essential.

Mercury Conjunct Chiron

Communication becomes vehicle for healing or re-wounding. Mercury lines intensify the urge to teach from wounds. The challenge involves sharing vulnerability without overwhelming others or traumatizing self through premature disclosure. Writing, speaking, and teaching about healing themes thrive on these lines when approached consciously.

Mars Square Chiron

Action and assertion trigger core wounds around anger, aggression, or victimization. Mars lines force working with wounded warrior patterns—either excessive aggression or inability to assert at all. Healing requires developing capacity for healthy assertion that neither wounds self nor others. Martial arts, therapy, or conscious anger work recommended.

Jupiter Opposition Chiron

Faith and meaning-making conflict with awareness of suffering. Jupiter lines force integration of optimism with realistic acknowledgment of pain. These locations benefit philosophers and spiritual teachers who've genuinely grappled with suffering rather than bypassing it with positive thinking. The wound becomes doorway to authentic wisdom.

Saturn Trine Chiron

Discipline and structure support healing work naturally. Saturn lines provide container for therapeutic process, making wounded healer work sustainable rather than overwhelming. These locations suit long-term therapy, healing practices, or teaching that requires maturity and boundaries. The trine makes difficult work manageable through patient effort.

Pluto Conjunct Chiron

Transformation through core wounding creates intense healing potential. Chiron or Pluto lines bring volcanic healing experiences—death and rebirth through engaging deepest wounds. These locations demand therapeutic support and should only be activated when ready for profound psychological work. The potential for transformation is enormous; so is the intensity.

The Chiron Return: Peak Healing Window

Chiron's orbital period is approximately 50-51 years, creating the Chiron return around age 50. This represents a critical life passage when the nature of your core wound and its potential as wisdom becomes fully apparent. Like nodal returns, Chiron returns intensify the significance of Chiron lines dramatically.

Chiron Return Strategic Timing:

Clients approaching or experiencing their Chiron return (ages 48-52) while living on Chiron lines often report profound revelations about the purpose of their suffering. What felt like random pain or personal failure reveals itself as preparation for specific teaching or healing work. The wound transforms from liability into qualification for service.

This period represents optimal timing for intentional Chiron work. Clients have enough life experience to understand their wounds deeply, yet sufficient vitality to transform that understanding into active service. Recommend Chiron lines during Chiron return years for clients ready to fully embody the wounded healer archetype. Avoid for clients lacking therapeutic support or spiritual practice.

Aspects to Part of Fortune

Part of Fortune represents natural luck, flow, and where good fortune comes easily. Planets aspecting your Part of Fortune carry fortunate qualities, creating lines where that planetary energy operates with particular grace and advantage.

Jupiter Sextile Part of Fortune

If your Jupiter sextiles your Part of Fortune, your Jupiter lines are doubly fortunate. Expansion, opportunity, and growth come with unusual ease. This is excellent for career development, education, travel, or any ventures requiring optimism and good fortune. The sextile requires conscious activation but provides reliable advantage when engaged.

Sun Conjunct Part of Fortune

Identity expression flows with natural ease and fortune. Sun lines bring opportunities aligned with authentic self-expression. Visibility and leadership feel natural rather than forced. These locations support being yourself while attracting good fortune through genuine presence. Excellent for career development requiring personal brand or charisma.

Venus Trine Part of Fortune

Love, pleasure, and aesthetic pursuits come easily. Venus lines are doubly fortunate for relationships, creative work, and financial abundance. Beauty attracts opportunity naturally. These locations support artists, creatives, relationship seekers, or anyone whose work involves aesthetics. The ease can create complacency—maintain active engagement.

Mars Square Part of Fortune

Action and assertion create friction with natural flow. Mars lines demand working for fortune rather than receiving it passively. This builds character and ensures earned success. The square prevents taking advantages for granted by requiring effort. Useful for developing discipline and drive, but won't feel as lucky as other Part of Fortune activations.

Saturn Conjunct Part of Fortune

Fortune requires structure, patience, and long-term effort. Saturn lines bring luck through discipline and maturity. Success comes slowly but endures. These locations suit building lasting foundations, developing mastery, or any work requiring sustained commitment. The fortune isn't immediate but compounds over time.

Part of Fortune and Annual Profections

Annual profections, an ancient timing technique, move the angles of your chart forward one sign per year of life. When the profected Ascendant activates a particular house, that house's themes dominate the year. Combining this with Part of Fortune astrocartography creates powerful timing strategies.

Strategic Profection Timing:

If your Part of Fortune occupies your 10th house and you enter a 10th house profection year, temporarily living on or traveling to Part of Fortune lines maximizes professional opportunity. The profection activates career themes; the Part of Fortune line provides natural flow and luck within those themes. The combination creates optimal conditions for advancement.

This technique works for any house profection. Second house year? Use Part of Fortune lines for financial opportunity. Seventh house year? Part of Fortune lines for fortunate partnerships. Calculate profection years by dividing current age by 12—the remainder determines which house is activated. Strategic temporary positioning during profection years amplifies natural luck.

Aspects to the Vertex

The Vertex represents fated encounters, destiny points, significant meetings with people or situations. Planets aspecting your Vertex carry a quality of fate or meant-to-be-ness. These planetary lines often bring significant encounters that feel destined or karmically arranged.

Venus Conjunct Vertex

If your Venus conjoins your Vertex, your Venus lines bring fated relationship encounters. People you meet on these lines often feel significant, destined, or like they were meant to enter your life. The relationships may or may not be easy, but they carry weight and meaning beyond ordinary connections.

Sun Square Vertex

Identity development conflicts with fated encounters. Sun lines bring people or situations that challenge self-expression, forcing growth through friction with destiny. These encounters feel significant but uncomfortable—they're meant to push you beyond current self-concept. The square creates transformation through destined challenge.

Mars Conjunct Vertex

Action triggers fated conflicts or passionate encounters. Mars lines bring people who challenge you, inspire assertiveness, or create situations requiring courage. The destiny involves learning appropriate use of will and aggression. Encounters feel intense, sometimes combative, always significant for developing healthy assertion.

Jupiter Trine Vertex

Fortunate destiny activation. Jupiter lines bring opportunities through synchronicity and fortunate timing. Teachers, mentors, or guides enter your life through apparent chance that feels orchestrated by benevolent forces. These locations support expansion through grace rather than effort. The destiny here involves growth through good fortune.

Saturn Opposition Vertex

Destined limitations or karmic responsibilities. Saturn lines bring fated encounters with authority, restriction, or serious commitment. The people or situations you meet teach maturity through necessity. These feel heavy, consequential, unavoidable—classic Saturn themes operating through Vertex destiny mechanism. Growth through accepting fated responsibility.

Pluto Conjunct Vertex

Transformative fated encounters of maximum intensity. Pluto lines bring people or situations that completely alter life trajectory. The encounters feel compulsive, powerful, often sexual or psychological. Destiny involves transformation through unavoidable intensity. These locations catalyze profound change through encounters you cannot ignore or escape.

Vertex Transit Activation Windows

While Vertex lines create relatively constant fated-encounter potential, specific transit periods amplify Vertex activation dramatically. When outer planets aspect your natal Vertex while you're living on Vertex lines, destiny experiences intensify significantly.

Strategic Vertex Transit Timing:

Jupiter transits to natal Vertex on Vertex lines: Fortunate meant-to-be opportunities multiply. Plan important ventures, relationship seeking, or career moves during these periods for maximum synchronistic support.

Saturn transits to natal Vertex on Vertex lines: Fated responsibilities or karmic encounters arrive. These feel serious, consequential, unavoidable. The meetings or situations demand maturity and long-term commitment.

Uranus transits to natal Vertex on Vertex lines: Sudden destined disruptions or revolutionary encounters. Life changes unexpectedly through people or situations that feel fated. The encounters liberate or destabilize depending on readiness for change.

Neptune transits to natal Vertex on Vertex lines: Spiritually significant encounters that may involve confusion, dissolution, or divine connection. Boundaries blur with fated people. The challenge involves discerning genuine spiritual connection from projection or delusion.

Pluto transits to natal Vertex on Vertex lines: Transformative encounters of maximum intensity and permanence. These meetings or situations completely remake life. The destiny involves death-rebirth transformation through unavoidable encounters.

Aspects to Juno

Juno governs committed partnership, marriage, and equal relationship dynamics. Planets aspecting Juno reveal what activates in partnerships and how partnership themes play out geographically. These aspects become critical for anyone seeking serious committed relationships or business partnerships.

Venus Trine Juno

Love and partnership align harmoniously. Venus lines support committed relationships that combine pleasure with lasting commitment. Attraction naturally evolves into partnership. These locations benefit relationship seeking or partnership work requiring both attraction and serious commitment. The ease can create complacency—maintain active partnership development.

Mars Square Juno

Action and assertion create power struggles in partnerships. Mars lines bring partnerships requiring constant negotiation around autonomy versus commitment. The friction serves growth if both parties commit to conscious work. Without awareness, creates repetitive conflicts around independence, anger, and assertion within relationship. Couples therapy recommended.

Sun Conjunct Juno

Identity and partnership fuse completely. Sun lines make partnership central to self-expression and purpose. You define yourself through committed relationship for better or worse. These locations attract partnerships that either support authentic identity or subsume it. The work involves maintaining self within partnership—challenging but potentially transformative.

Saturn Trine Juno

Maturity and structure support partnership naturally. Saturn lines bring serious, committed partnerships built on realistic foundations. The relationships endure through patient work and mutual responsibility. These locations suit long-term partnership development, business partnerships requiring trust, or marriage with clear boundaries and commitments.

Pluto Conjunct Juno

Transformative intensity in partnerships. Juno lines bring relationships involving power, control, obsession, and profound transformation. The partnerships completely remake you through intensity that borders on compulsion. Therapeutic support essential for navigating power dynamics without becoming destructive. Maximum potential for growth and danger.

Aspects to Black Moon Lilith

Lilith represents rejected aspects of self, shadow material demanding integration, and authentic power refusing domestication. Aspects to Lilith reveal which planetary themes involve shadow work, rejection patterns, and reclaiming authentic power.

Sun Conjunct Lilith

Identity includes rejected, shadow, or socially unacceptable aspects. Sun lines demand authentic self-expression refusing compromise for social approval. You attract strong reactions—magnetic attraction or fierce rejection. The work involves owning your power without becoming destructive or isolated. These locations suit people ready to be controversial or unconventional.

Moon Square Lilith

Emotional needs conflict with rejected shadow material. Moon lines force working with dark emotions, rage, or needs considered unacceptable. The friction creates opportunities for emotional authenticity beyond social conditioning. Requires therapeutic support for integrating shadow emotions without becoming overwhelmed or destructive.

Venus Conjunct Lilith

Love and sexuality include raw, undomesticated power. Venus lines bring relationships refusing conventional relationship norms. You attract unconventional partnerships or express sexuality in ways society may judge. The work involves authentic relating that honors wild feminine (or masculine) power while maintaining ethics and boundaries.

Mars Trine Lilith

Assertion and shadow power align naturally. Mars lines support authentic action refusing social control or limitation. You access primal will and courage that doesn't require permission. These locations benefit creatives, entrepreneurs, or anyone whose work demands unconventional assertiveness. The trine makes wild power productive rather than destructive.

Aspects to Ceres

Ceres governs nurturing, nourishment, mothering, and grief through loss. Aspects to Ceres reveal how planetary themes intertwine with caregiving, food, body image, and processing loss. These aspects become particularly relevant during grief periods or for those in nurturing professions.

Moon Trine Ceres

Emotional nurturing flows naturally. Moon lines support caregiving, mothering, or healing work involving emotional nourishment. Home becomes sanctuary for processing grief and providing care. These locations benefit therapists, counselors, parents, or anyone whose work involves tending emotional needs. The ease makes sustainable caregiving possible.

Saturn Square Ceres

Discipline conflicts with nurturing needs. Saturn lines create friction between self-care and productivity, between feeding self and feeding others. The square forces developing sustainable caregiving that includes boundaries. Without consciousness, creates depletion through over-giving or restriction through excessive control. Balance requires conscious effort.

Venus Conjunct Ceres

Love and nourishment fuse. Venus lines make beauty and pleasure inseparable from nurturing. Food becomes aesthetic experience. Caregiving includes sensual pleasure. These locations support chefs, food artists, or anyone whose work combines aesthetics with nourishment. The challenge involves potential eating disorders or body image issues requiring therapeutic attention.

Aspects to Pallas Athene

Pallas governs wisdom, strategy, pattern recognition, and creative intelligence. Aspects to Pallas reveal which planetary themes benefit from strategic thinking and where pattern-seeing abilities activate most powerfully.

Mercury Sextile Pallas

Communication and strategy combine productively. Mercury lines enhance pattern recognition and strategic communication. You see connections others miss and articulate complex patterns clearly. These locations benefit consultants, strategists, therapists working with systemic patterns, or anyone requiring both intelligence and clear communication.

Jupiter Square Pallas

Vision conflicts with strategy. Jupiter lines create tension between big-picture thinking and practical planning. The square forces integrating philosophy with execution. Without consciousness, creates brilliant ideas without follow-through or rigid plans without vision. The friction serves growth when both are honored.

Mars Trine Pallas

Action and strategy align naturally. Mars lines support strategic action and tactical execution. You devise plans and implement them effectively. These locations benefit military strategy, business competition, game design, or any field requiring both strategic thinking and decisive action. The combination creates practical wisdom.

Aspects to Vesta

Vesta governs devotion, focus, sacred practice, and commitment to what matters most. Aspects to Vesta reveal which planetary themes require dedicated focus and where spiritual practice becomes most potent.

Saturn Trine Vesta

Discipline and devotion support each other naturally. Saturn lines create ideal conditions for sustained spiritual practice, dedicated work, or long-term focus on what's sacred. Structure serves devotion rather than restricting it. These locations support monastics, researchers, artists developing mastery, or anyone committed to decades-long work.

Venus Square Vesta

Pleasure and devotion create tension. Venus lines force choosing between relationship/pleasure and sacred solitary work. The square demands integrating both rather than sacrificing one for the other. The challenge involves maintaining devotion to sacred work while allowing healthy relationship and pleasure. Balance requires conscious effort and clear priorities.

Sun Conjunct Vesta

Identity and sacred devotion fuse. Sun lines make spiritual practice or dedicated work central to self-expression. You ARE what you're devoted to. These locations support people whose purpose involves complete dedication to craft, spiritual path, or sacred work. The intensity can create isolation—maintain balance between devotion and human connection.

Aspects to Eros and Psyche

Eros governs passionate desire and creative drive. Psyche governs soul development and deep psychological integration. Together they represent the mythic journey toward wholeness through trials and ultimate union.

Mars Conjunct Eros

Action and passionate desire fuse intensely. Mars lines bring volcanic creative and sexual energy. Pursuit of what you desire becomes consuming. These locations suit artists needing powerful creative drive, or anyone whose work requires sustained passionate engagement. The challenge involves directing intensity constructively rather than compulsively.

Venus Trine Eros

Love and passionate desire align naturally. Venus lines combine attraction with genuine desire, creating relationships or creative work fueled by authentic passion. The trine makes passionate pursuit feel natural rather than compulsive. These locations support creative projects requiring sustained desire or relationships combining love with ongoing passion.

Saturn Trine Psyche

Discipline supports soul work naturally. Saturn lines create structure for deep psychological integration and spiritual development. Therapy, shadow work, or spiritual practice becomes sustainable through patient effort. These locations benefit long-term psychological work requiring commitment and maturity.

Pluto Conjunct Psyche

Transformation and soul development fuse completely. Psyche lines bring volcanic inner work requiring complete transformation. The psychological and spiritual demands are intense, potentially overwhelming without adequate support. Only recommend for clients actively engaged in therapy or spiritual practice with strong containers for processing intensity.

Aspects to Arabic Lots

The Lot of Spirit, Lot of Eros, and Lot of Marriage represent calculated destiny points combining three chart factors. Aspects to these lots reveal which planetary themes intertwine with spiritual purpose, passionate desire, and partnership destiny.

Jupiter Trine Lot of Spirit

Expansion and spiritual purpose align naturally. Jupiter lines support growth through living according to soul values. Teaching, philosophy, and spiritual work flourish. These locations benefit anyone seeking to integrate success with purpose, abundance with meaning. The trine makes purposeful living feel fortunate rather than sacrificial.

Saturn Square Lot of Spirit

Responsibility conflicts with spiritual purpose. Saturn lines force working hard for meaningful living rather than expecting ease. Purpose requires discipline and patience. The square prevents spiritual bypassing by demanding practical application of values. The friction serves integrity—purpose must be lived, not just philosophized.

Mars Conjunct Lot of Eros

Action and destiny-level desire fuse. Mars lines bring magnetic pursuit of what you're meant to desire. The passion feels fated, compulsive, unavoidable. These locations catalyze creative projects or relationships you're destined to pursue. The challenge involves conscious direction of powerful desire rather than unconscious compulsion.

Venus Conjunct Lot of Marriage

Love and partnership destiny fuse. Venus lines bring relationships that feel meant-to-be and naturally evolve toward commitment. The people you meet carry karmic significance for partnership themes. These locations benefit marriage seeking or business partnership development. The relationships feel fortunate and fated simultaneously.

Integrating Special Point Aspects

When evaluating a planetary line, check not just major planetary aspects but also aspects to these special points. They add layers of meaning and purpose to line experiences. A Venus line becomes more complex and significant when you realize Venus also aspects your North Node (evolutionary direction), trines your Chiron (healing potential), and sextiles your Part of Fortune (natural advantage).

Understanding these additional connections helps you appreciate why certain lines feel particularly meaningful or fated beyond what simple planetary interpretation suggests. The special points add soul-level significance to geographic activations, transforming locations from merely pleasant or challenging into places of destiny, healing, and evolutionary unfoldment.

Professional Assessment Protocol

When consulting professionally with clients about special point aspects, use systematic methodology to avoid overwhelming complexity while capturing essential patterns.

Five-Step Special Point Assessment

STEP 1: Identify relevant special points for client's question. Relationship questions? Check Juno, Vertex, Lot of Marriage. Purpose questions? Check North Node, Lot of Spirit. Healing questions? Check Chiron, Psyche.

STEP 2: Map all aspects to relevant special points. Note aspect types, orbs, and aspecting planets. Tight aspects (0-3 degrees) dominate more than wide aspects (6-10 degrees).

STEP 3: Track upcoming transits to special points for next 12-24 months. Identify windows when transits activate natal special points while client is on those lines. This creates optimal or challenging timing windows.

STEP 4: Synthesize patterns rather than listing individual aspects. 'Your Venus aspects Chiron, North Node, and Part of Fortune, creating lines where relationships support healing, evolutionary growth, and natural fortune' communicates more clearly than describing each aspect separately.

STEP 5: Provide timing guidance based on returns and transits. Recommend activating Chiron lines during Chiron return years. Suggest nodal lines during nodal returns. Time Part of Fortune activation with profection years. Strategic timing amplifies results dramatically.

Orb Considerations for Special Points

Tight aspects (0-3 degrees) to special points create consistent, reliable activation. Wide aspects (6-10 degrees) create conditional activation that emerges during relevant transits or in specific circumstances. Apply the same orb principles used for planetary aspects.

Example: Venus at 15 degrees Libra trine Chiron at 16 degrees Gemini (1-degree orb) creates strong, consistent healing-through-relationship activation on Venus lines. Venus at 15 degrees Libra trine Chiron at 23 degrees Gemini (8-degree orb) creates occasional healing potential that fully activates during Chiron transits or when consciously engaged. Both matter, but tight orbs dominate experience.

When to Emphasize vs Minimize Special Points

Not every consultation requires detailed special point analysis. Emphasize special points when directly relevant to client questions. Minimize or omit when planetary aspects tell the complete story.

Emphasize Special Points When

- Client asks about soul purpose, life direction, or meaning (North Node, Lot of Spirit)
- Client is processing grief, loss, or healing wounds (Chiron, Ceres, Psyche)
- Client seeks serious committed partnerships (Juno, Lot of Marriage)
- Client reports synchronistic or fated experiences (Vertex)
- Client is near major returns (Nodal return ages 18, 37, 56; Chiron return age 50)
- Planetary aspects alone don't explain reported experiences

Minimize Special Points When

- Client asks basic location questions answered by planetary lines
- Client is new to astrology and learning foundations

• Planetary aspects tell complete story without additional complexity

• Client shows signs of overwhelm with technical information

• Special points don't aspect relevant planets for client's situation

Aspect activation of special points represents sophisticated astrocartography practice requiring strong foundation in both traditional astrology and planetary astrocartography. Master planetary aspects before adding special points. Use special points to deepen and refine interpretation rather than replace core planetary analysis. When skillfully applied, special point aspects reveal soul-level dimensions of geographic experience that transform astrocartography from practical tool into wisdom practice.

Chapter Ten

T-Squares: Navigating Maximum Pressure Points

My friend Amanda thought I was crazy when I suggested she move to Denver on her Mars line. 'You want me to go to my Mars line? Are you trying to kill me?' She had a Moon-Saturn-Mars T-Square, and Mars was the apex—the pressure point receiving tension from both sides. Every astrologer she'd consulted had told her to avoid Mars lines like the plague. Too intense. Too much pressure. Guaranteed burnout.

But here's what those astrologers missed: Amanda had been avoiding Mars her entire life. She was brilliant, capable, driven—but terrified of her own anger and assertion. The Moon-Saturn opposition kept her trapped between emotional needs and harsh self-discipline, never finding resolution. The Mars apex was exactly what she needed to develop. Not someday. Now.

She moved to Denver. It was exactly as hard as I'd warned her it would be. Two years of relentless Mars lessons—learning to assert boundaries, fight for what mattered, channel anger constructively instead of turning it inward. She cried, she raged, she wanted to quit every few months. But she stayed. And something remarkable happened. The T-Square that had felt like a curse her whole life became her greatest strength. That apex planet she'd feared? It became her superpower.

T-Squares represent one of the most challenging and growth-producing configurations in astrology. Three planets form two squares and one opposition, creating a triangle of tension with one planet at the apex receiving pressure from both sides. When you activate any line involved in your T-Square, you activate the entire pattern, bringing all three planetary energies into intense focus. This chapter explores how to work with T-Square activation consciously and when this configuration creates breakthrough versus breakdown.

Understanding T-Square Dynamics

T-Squares create a sense of being caught between opposing forces with no easy resolution. Two planets oppose each other, creating a polarity that needs balancing. A third planet squares both, creating a focal point where the tension concentrates. This apex planet becomes the key to working with the entire pattern. It's simultaneously the point of greatest pressure and greatest potential for resolution.

The two planets in opposition represent competing needs or drives. You can't simply choose one side and ignore the other—both ends of the polarity demand attention. The apex planet represents the area where you must develop new capacity to handle the opposition's tension. You can't resolve the opposition by choosing one side. You must develop the apex planet's qualities to hold both ends of the polarity simultaneously.

T-Squares exist in three modalities: cardinal (initiation, action), fixed (persistence, resistance), or mutable (adaptation, changeability). The modality reveals how the tension manifests. Cardinal T-Squares create crisis through competing initiatives and demands for action. Fixed T-Squares create stubbornness and resistance to necessary change. Mutable T-Squares create scattered energy and difficulty maintaining focus.

Living on the Apex Planet Line

The apex planet line is the most intense T-Square activation. This line brings maximum pressure because you're living at the focal point where all the tension concentrates. However, it's also where the greatest growth potential exists. If you're ready to develop that planetary capacity, the apex line provides non-stop opportunities for practice and integration.

Characteristics of Apex Planet Activation

• Constant demand for that planet's expression and development

• Feeling pressured or overwhelmed by responsibility to handle the opposition's tension

• Rapid skill development in that planetary area through necessity

• Potential for burnout if support is inadequate or self-awareness insufficient

• Breakthrough moments when the pattern suddenly integrates and flows

• Sense of being tested repeatedly in the same themes until mastery develops

Example: Michael's Moon-Saturn-Mars T-Square

Michael has Moon at 12 degrees Cancer opposing Saturn at 14 degrees Capricorn, with Mars at 13 degrees Aries squaring both. This creates a cardinal T-Square with Mars as the apex. The Moon-Saturn opposition represents the tension between emotional needs (Moon) and responsible limitation (Saturn), between vulnerability and self-sufficiency, between needing care and being stoic.

Mars at the apex means Michael must develop assertive action to handle this emotional-structural tension. He can't simply be emotional (Moon) or simply be disciplined (Saturn). He must learn to assert himself appropriately, to take action that honors both emotional authenticity and mature responsibility. This is not easy. Mars wants direct expression. The Moon-Saturn opposition keeps pulling him between too much feeling and too much control.

When Michael relocated to Seattle on his Mars Midheaven line, the entire T-Square activated intensely. His career (Midheaven) became the arena where Moon-Saturn-Mars dynamics played out daily. He felt pressured to perform and achieve (Saturn) while managing emotional vulnerability (Moon) through assertive action (Mars). The intensity was exhausting but ultimately transformative. Seattle forced him to develop the Mars qualities he'd been avoiding, creating breakthrough in both emotional maturity and professional effectiveness.

The key insight: Michael didn't fail on his Mars line. The pressure was exactly what his T-Square needed for integration. Less intense locations would have allowed continued avoidance. Seattle's demands catalyzed growth that couldn't happen in comfort zones. Two years of intensity created capacities that will serve him for life.

Living on Opposition Planet Lines

Activating either planet in the opposition (the base of the T-Square) brings that polarity into sharp focus while also activating the apex planet's pressure. You experience one end of the opposition more directly while the other end projects outward or manifests through circumstances. The apex planet remains as constant background tension requiring attention.

Example: Sarah's Sun-Pluto-Uranus T-Square

Sarah has Sun at 19 degrees Aries opposing Pluto at 14 degrees Libra, with Uranus at 16 degrees Cancer squaring both. When she moved to Portland on her Moon line (close to her Uranus position), she expected emotional security and home focus. Instead, the

T-Square activated powerfully. Her home and emotional life became the arena for Sun-Pluto transformation work.

Identity crises (Sun) and power struggles (Pluto) played out through domestic situations, requiring constant innovative solutions (Uranus apex). The experience was intense but ultimately liberating. Sarah developed unprecedented capacity for emotional revolution, for breaking free from stuck patterns, for allowing transformation without losing her core identity. The Uranus apex planet required her to find new, unconventional ways to be both herself and willing to transform.

Portland on her Moon-Uranus line forced this integration. The location provided the catalyst. Sarah's consciousness and commitment to growth determined whether the catalyst created breakthrough or breakdown. She chose therapeutic support, community connection, and spiritual practice. These containers allowed the T-Square pressure to forge strength rather than create fragmentation.

The Missing Leg: Empty Point Opposite Apex

T-Squares have an empty point directly opposite the apex planet. This empty point, sometimes called the missing leg, represents the release valve for T-Square pressure. Developing the qualities of the sign and house where this point falls provides relief and resolution for the entire pattern.

In Michael's T-Square with Mars at the apex in Aries, the missing leg is in Libra. This suggests that developing partnership skills, diplomatic communication, and cooperative relating provides the outlet for his Mars-Moon-Saturn tension. When he learned to work with others rather than pushing independently, the T-Square pressure decreased significantly. Seattle helped him develop these Libra qualities through collaborative work projects.

The missing leg doesn't eliminate T-Square tension—it provides constructive channels for the energy. Think of it as the overflow valve that prevents explosive buildup. Geographic locations that activate the missing leg degree or sign provide natural relief while still working with the configuration.

T-Square Timing Considerations

Transits to T-Squares are particularly significant because one transit can activate all three planets simultaneously. When Saturn transits any point in your T-Square, it triggers the entire configuration. This creates periods of maximum pressure and maximum breakthrough potential. Understanding this timing helps you choose when to be on T-Square lines versus when to seek easier locations.

Strategic Timing Guidelines

Harmonious transits (trines, sextiles) to T-Square points provide support for working with the pattern. Jupiter trining your apex planet while you're on that line creates optimism and expansion that makes the pressure more workable. The challenge remains but feels manageable and meaningful rather than crushing.

Challenging transits (squares, oppositions) to T-Square points intensify already intense patterns. Pluto squaring your T-Square planets while you're living on one of those lines creates transformation through crisis that can be overwhelming without extraordinary support. The pattern demands conscious engagement during difficult transits or risk breakdown.

Consider transit density—multiple challenging transits to T-Square planets simultaneously demands retreat to gentler locations. One challenging transit with good support systems might catalyze growth. Five simultaneous challenging transits creates potential crisis regardless of consciousness or preparation.

Use lunar returns and progressed Moon to track shorter timing cycles. When progressed Moon aspects T-Square planets, emotional themes intensify for 2-3 years. Plan T-Square line relocations during supportive progressed Moon periods rather than challenging ones.

Modality-Specific T-Square Strategies

Cardinal T-Squares (Aries, Cancer, Libra, Capricorn)

Cardinal T-Squares create crisis through competing initiatives and action demands. These configurations produce driven, achievement-oriented people who struggle with work-life balance and knowing when to stop pushing. On cardinal T-Square lines, the pressure to initiate, achieve, and make things happen intensifies dramatically.

Strategic approach: Use cardinal T-Square lines for time-limited intensive projects with clear endpoints. The configuration provides powerful drive for accomplishment. Set firm boundaries on work hours and achievement pressure. Without limits, cardinal T-Square activation creates burnout through endless initiation.

Fixed T-Squares (Taurus, Leo, Scorpio, Aquarius)

Fixed T-Squares create stubbornness and resistance to necessary change. These configurations produce persistent people who struggle with flexibility and knowing when to release. On fixed T-Square lines, the tendency to dig in and resist intensifies, creating potential for stuck energy and blocked growth.

Strategic approach: Use fixed T-Square lines when you need sustained commitment to difficult work requiring persistence. The configuration provides powerful staying power. However, build in regular check-ins with trusted advisors who can identify when persistence has become destructive stubbornness. Fixed T-Square activation requires conscious flexibility work.

Mutable T-Squares (Gemini, Virgo, Sagittarius, Pisces)

Mutable T-Squares create scattered energy and difficulty maintaining focus. These configurations produce adaptable people who struggle with commitment and follow-through. On mutable T-Square lines, the tendency to scatter and avoid finality intensifies, creating potential for chronic incompletion.

Strategic approach: Use mutable T-Square lines when you need flexibility and adaptation to changing circumstances. The configuration provides powerful versatility. However, implement strong structures and accountability systems. Mutable T-Square activation requires external organization to channel the adaptable energy productively.

When to Choose vs Avoid T-Square Lines

Choose T-Square Lines When

- You're ready for intensive growth work and conscious development
- You have strong support systems in place (therapy, community, mentorship)
- You're willing to develop apex planet capacities through sustained pressure
- Other areas of life are relatively stable, providing foundation
- Transits are supportive (harmonious aspects to T-Square planets)
- You have clear growth goals aligned with the configuration's demands
- You're in a life phase where challenge serves your larger purpose

Avoid T-Square Lines When

- You're in active crisis or multiple life areas are unstable
- You lack adequate support systems or resources
- Multiple challenging transits are hitting T-Square planets simultaneously

- You need rest, recovery, or gentle integration
- You're not ready to engage the apex planet's challenges consciously
- Health (physical or mental) is compromised
- You're seeking ease rather than growth through pressure

Professional Guidance for T-Square Consultations

When clients have T-Squares, assess readiness before recommending activation. Someone with therapy practice and strong self-awareness might thrive on T-Square challenges. Someone in active crisis needs gentler options. Your role includes helping clients understand the difference between growth-producing challenge and overwhelming crisis.

Explain T-Squares clearly without creating fear. These aren't curses or permanent limitations—they're growth engines that demand consciousness. Clients with T-Squares often report their greatest achievements and most meaningful growth occurred through working with the configuration rather than avoiding it.

Help clients identify their T-Square's missing leg and develop those qualities. This practical guidance provides actionable steps rather than just describing difficulty. If someone has Mars apex with Libra missing leg, suggest partnership skills development, collaborative projects, and diplomatic communication practice.

Track clients' T-Square transit timing carefully. When major outer planets aspect T-Square configurations, check in proactively. Your awareness of timing allows intervention before crisis escalates. Recommend support system strengthening before intense periods rather than crisis management during them.

T-Squares represent astrocartography's most challenging and rewarding territory. These configurations create pressure that forges character, develops capacity, and catalyzes growth impossible in comfort zones. With conscious engagement, adequate support, and strategic timing, T-Square line activation becomes transformative rather than traumatic. The key lies in understanding your unique pattern, knowing your readiness level, choosing timing wisely, and maintaining awareness throughout the process.

Chapter Eleven

Grand Trines: The Gift and the Trap of Ease

Tyler was the most naturally gifted writer I'd ever met. Fire Grand Trine—Sun in Aries, Moon in Leo, Jupiter in Sagittarius. Words poured out of him effortlessly. Brilliant ideas, inspiring vision, infectious enthusiasm. Everyone who read his work said the same thing: 'This is amazing. When's the book coming out?'

The book never came out. Tyler would start writing with tremendous passion, produce fifty magnificent pages, then get excited about a different project and abandon the first one. He had seventeen unfinished novels, countless abandoned screenplays, and a trail of disappointed editors. His Fire Grand Trine gave him all the creative fire anyone could want. What it didn't give him was the discipline to finish anything.

When he moved to Austin on his Moon line, activating the entire Grand Trine, I thought maybe the emotional connection (Moon) would help him commit. Instead, the ease intensified. More ideas. More enthusiasm. More starting. Still no finishing. It took hiring a Virgo business manager—someone with strong Earth energy who could impose external structure—before Tyler finally completed a project. Same Grand Trine, same natural talent. But talent without discipline is just a pleasant waste.

Grand Trines connect three planets in a perfect equilateral triangle, approximately 120 degrees apart, all in the same element. This configuration creates natural flow, ease, and talent so effortless it can become unconscious. Unlike T-Squares that demand development through pressure, Grand Trines offer gifts that require conscious direction to reach their potential. When you activate any line involved in your Grand Trine, you activate all three planets simultaneously, creating flowing energy that can manifest as either genius or waste depending on consciousness and effort.

Understanding Grand Trine Dynamics

Grand Trines create harmony through elemental consistency. All three planets operate in the same element—Fire, Earth, Air, or Water—creating natural understanding and cooperation between them. The 120-degree trine aspects promote flow rather than friction. Energy moves easily between the three points without resistance or conflict.

The gift of Grand Trines is also their trap. Ease can create complacency. Talent that comes naturally often goes undeveloped because there's no pressure forcing practice and refinement. People with Grand Trines frequently underachieve relative to their potential because they've never needed to work hard in that elemental area. The very absence of challenge prevents development of discipline and focused effort.

Grand Trines work best when connected to challenging aspects in the chart. A Grand Trine with a planet also involved in a T-Square creates natural talent that must develop under pressure. The challenge provides motivation; the Grand Trine provides capacity. Without any challenging aspects, Grand Trines can create gifted people who never quite fulfill their promise.

Grand Trine Activation in Astrocartography

With Grand Trines, it doesn't matter which planetary line you activate—all three planets wake up together because they're all connected by harmonious aspects. Moving to your Sun line activates the Sun-Moon-Jupiter Grand Trine entirely if you have one. The ease distributes evenly across all three points rather than concentrating at one location.

This creates both opportunity and challenge for strategic planning. You have three or more potential locations (depending on how many lines each planet has) that could activate the Grand Trine. The question becomes which location provides the right combination of flow and structure to channel the ease productively.

Grand Trine Activation Principles

- All three planets activate regardless of which line you're on
- The element's quality pervades the entire experience
- Ease flows naturally but requires conscious direction
- Locations need some structure or challenge to prevent waste
- Multiple line options exist—choose strategically
- Success depends on effort despite natural talent

Element-Specific Grand Trine Strategies

Fire Grand Trines (Aries, Leo, Sagittarius)

Fire Grand Trines create natural confidence, enthusiasm, and spontaneous action. These configurations produce people with inspiring vision and infectious optimism. On Fire Grand Trine lines, creative fire burns brightly and initiative comes easily. The challenge involves maintaining discipline and follow-through when inspiration fades.

Fire Grand Trine gifts: Natural leadership and charisma, creative inspiration that flows abundantly, confidence that attracts opportunity, enthusiasm that motivates others, ability to start projects with bold vision, faith in possibilities and potential.

Fire Grand Trine shadows: Starting without finishing, scattered creative energy, overconfidence without skill development, burning out from excessive enthusiasm, difficulty with sustained effort, ignoring practical considerations, grandiose plans without realistic assessment.

Strategic Application:

Use Fire Grand Trine lines for inspiration, creative breakthrough, and bold initiative. However, pair Fire line activation with strong external structure. Join accountability groups, hire project managers, establish rigorous schedules. Fire Grand Trines need Earth energy (structure, discipline) to ground their vision. Choose Fire line locations that include practical demands or disciplined communities that channel enthusiasm productively.

Example: David's Fire Grand Trine

David has Sun in Aries, Moon in Leo, and Jupiter in Sagittarius forming a Fire Grand Trine. He relocated to Austin on his Moon line, activating the entire configuration. His emotional life (Moon) became infused with confidence, creativity, and optimistic vision. He started three businesses in two years, each launched with tremendous enthusiasm and inspiring vision.

The problem: none of the businesses succeeded because David moved to the next exciting idea before establishing sustainable systems. The Fire Grand Trine provided endless inspiration but no discipline. After recognizing the pattern, David hired a business manager with strong Virgo placements who implemented structure and accountability. The same Austin location with added Earth energy (the manager) transformed scattered fire into focused achievement.

Earth Grand Trines (Taurus, Virgo, Capricorn)

Earth Grand Trines create natural practical manifestation, material success, and grounded stability. These configurations produce people who build sustainable structures and accumulate resources steadily. On Earth Grand Trine lines, material success flows naturally and practical work feels effortless. The challenge involves avoiding excessive focus on form over meaning.

Earth Grand Trine gifts: Natural material success and financial stability, ability to manifest goals practically, grounded common sense and realistic assessment, patient persistence and sustainable effort, skill in resource management, appreciation for quality and craftsmanship.

Earth Grand Trine shadows: Materialism without spiritual depth, excessive caution and risk aversion, attachment to security over growth, missing opportunities through conservative approach, becoming too focused on practical concerns, resistance to necessary change, valuing stability over meaning.

Strategic Application:

Use Earth Grand Trine lines for building sustainable material success and establishing practical foundations. However, ensure spiritual or creative practices prevent excessive materialism. Earth Grand Trines need Fire energy (vision, inspiration) or Water energy (emotional depth) to balance pragmatic focus. Choose Earth line locations that include cultural richness, artistic communities, or spiritual centers that add meaning to material achievement.

Example: Jennifer's Earth Grand Trine

Jennifer has Venus in Taurus, Mars in Virgo, and Saturn in Capricorn forming an Earth Grand Trine. She relocated to Portland on her Venus line, activating the entire configuration. Her capacity for manifesting material success became remarkable—she built a profitable business, purchased property, and accumulated substantial savings within three years.

However, Jennifer found herself increasingly unhappy despite material success. The Earth Grand Trine created sustainable wealth but no deeper meaning. She joined a meditation community and began volunteer work with environmental organizations. These Water and Fire elements (emotional depth, inspired purpose) balanced the Earth Grand Trine's material focus, creating fulfillment alongside success.

Air Grand Trines (Gemini, Libra, Aquarius)

Air Grand Trines create natural mental brilliance, social grace, and communicative ease. These configurations produce people with quick minds and strong networking abilities. On Air Grand Trine lines, ideas flow abundantly and social connections form effortlessly. The challenge involves developing emotional depth beyond intellectual understanding.

Air Grand Trine gifts: Brilliant intellectual capacity and quick thinking, natural social grace and networking skill, clear communication across diverse groups, ability to see multiple perspectives, innovative ideas and solutions, understanding of systems and patterns.

Air Grand Trine shadows: Intellectualizing emotions without feeling them, social superficiality without depth, scattering mental energy across too many interests, difficulty committing to single path, living in head rather than body, avoiding emotional vulnerability through analysis, detachment from instinct and intuition.

Strategic Application:

Use Air Grand Trine lines for intellectual work, writing, teaching, and social networking. However, establish practices that develop emotional and physical intelligence. Air Grand Trines need Water energy (emotional depth) and Earth energy (embodied presence) to balance mental focus. Choose Air line locations that include body-based practices (dance, martial arts, yoga) or emotional depth work (therapy, intimate relationships) that ground the mental brilliance.

Example: Marcus's Air Grand Trine

Marcus has Mercury in Gemini, Venus in Libra, and Uranus in Aquarius forming an Air Grand Trine. He relocated to San Francisco on his Mercury line, activating the entire configuration. His intellectual and social capacities flourished—he wrote prolifically, networked brilliantly, and developed innovative ideas continuously.

Friends noticed Marcus lived entirely in his mind, rarely connecting emotionally or physically. He began intensive therapy and joined a men's group focused on embodied practices. These Water and Earth elements (emotional honesty, physical presence) brought depth to his Air Grand Trine brilliance, creating more meaningful relationships and work grounded in human experience rather than just clever ideas.

Water Grand Trines (Cancer, Scorpio, Pisces)

Water Grand Trines create natural emotional depth, intuitive understanding, and psychic sensitivity. These configurations produce people with profound empathy and spiritual connection. On Water Grand Trine lines, emotional and spiritual experiences flow naturally. The challenge involves maintaining boundaries and developing practical skills beyond feeling and intuition.

Water Grand Trine gifts: Deep emotional intelligence and empathy, natural psychic and intuitive abilities, capacity for spiritual experience and mystical states, understanding of unconscious patterns, healing presence and compassion, artistic sensitivity, ability to create emotional safety.

Water Grand Trine shadows: Emotional overwhelm and lack of boundaries, absorption of others' feelings without discernment, difficulty with practical action and material world, escapism through spiritual bypassing, victim consciousness and learned helplessness, excessive sensitivity creating paralysis, drowning in emotion without clarity.

Strategic Application:

Use Water Grand Trine lines for healing work, creative arts, spiritual practice, and therapeutic careers. However, establish strong boundaries and practical skills. Water Grand Trines need Fire energy (clear direction) and Earth energy (grounded action) to channel emotional depth productively. Choose Water line locations that include structured practices (martial arts, formal meditation) or practical demands that prevent emotional overwhelm.

Example: Lisa's Water Grand Trine

Lisa has Moon in Cancer, Venus in Scorpio, and Neptune in Pisces forming a Water Grand Trine. She relocated to Santa Fe on her Neptune line, activating the entire configuration. Her spiritual and emotional capacities became remarkable—she accessed profound mystical states, felt others' pain acutely, and created deeply moving artwork.

However, Lisa struggled with practical life. She couldn't maintain employment, failed to pay bills on time, and absorbed others' suffering to the point of incapacity. She began studying business skills and established firm schedules and boundaries. These Earth and Fire elements (practical discipline, clear direction) allowed her Water Grand Trine gifts to manifest sustainably through successful healing practice rather than dysfunctional overwhelm.

When Challenging Configurations Intersect Grand Trines

Some charts have both Grand Trines and challenging configurations (T-Squares, oppositions, hard aspects). These charts create interesting dynamics where natural talent meets necessary pressure. The Grand Trine provides capacity; the challenging aspects provide motivation. This combination often produces high achievement because ease is channeled through challenge toward concrete goals.

Example: Charts with Multiple Configurations

Rachel has a Fire Grand Trine (Sun-Mars-Jupiter) and a T-Square (Moon-Saturn-Uranus). Her Fire Grand Trine provides creative inspiration and confident initiative. Her T-Square demands emotional maturation through innovative approaches to security. When she activates Grand Trine lines, the creative fire flows but the T-Square ensures she channels it toward meaningful development rather than scattered enthusiasm.

The key: activate lines that engage both configurations strategically. Rachel's Mars line activates both the Fire Grand Trine (Mars trines Sun and Jupiter) and the T-Square's emotional work (Moon-Saturn-Uranus demands). The location provides both flow and challenge—ideal for maximum growth and achievement.

Timing Grand Trine Activation

Grand Trine timing focuses on adding external challenge or structure during activation periods. Pure Grand Trine ease without pressure rarely produces excellence. Strategic timing involves choosing periods when transits add constructive challenge to natural flow.

Optimal Timing Windows

- Saturn transiting Grand Trine planets: Adds discipline and structure to natural talent, perfect for building mastery
- Challenging transits to non-Grand-Trine planets: External pressure channels ease toward goals
- Jupiter transiting Grand Trine planets: Expands natural gifts but requires conscious effort to prevent waste
- Outer planet squares/oppositions: Creates productive tension that motivates Grand Trine development
- Avoid relocating to Grand Trine lines during only harmonious transits—too much ease creates complacency

Professional Guidance for Grand Trine Consultations

When clients have Grand Trines, address both the gifts and the shadows honestly. Many people with Grand Trines underachieve because nobody explained that ease requires conscious direction. Your role includes celebrating natural talents while providing realistic assessment of what's needed for those talents to reach potential.

Help clients understand that Grand Trine lines work best with external structure or internal discipline. Recommend accountability systems, structured practices, or locations with built-in demands that prevent waste of natural gifts. Grand Trine activation without consciousness creates pleasant mediocrity; with consciousness creates extraordinary achievement.

Look for charts where Grand Trines connect to challenging aspects. These clients have natural talent and motivation—they often achieve remarkable success when shown how to channel ease through challenge. Point out which lines activate both configurations for maximum strategic benefit.

Grand Trines represent astrocartography's most pleasant trap. These configurations offer genuine gifts and natural talents that can manifest as either wasted potential or extraordinary achievement depending entirely on consciousness and effort. With clear understanding, strategic activation, and willingness to add structure to flow, Grand Trine lines become platforms for excellence rather than comfortable mediocrity. The ease is real; what you do with that ease determines everything.

Chapter Twelve

Stelliums: Concentrated Power and Strategic Direction

I knew within five minutes of meeting Jessica that she had a Scorpio stellium. The intensity was unmistakable—that penetrating gaze, the way she cut through superficial conversation straight to the depths, the palpable sense of power barely contained beneath the surface. When I pulled up her chart, there they were: Sun, Mercury, Venus, and Mars all clustered in Scorpio in her 8th house. She wasn't just Scorpionic. She was Scorpio on steroids.

Jessica came to me because she felt like she was drowning. 'I can't do small talk. I can't do shallow. Everyone says I'm too much, too intense, too deep. Should I try to be more... normal?' I looked at that four-planet Scorpio stellium and wanted to laugh. Normal? She could no more be normal than the ocean could be a puddle. Her concentration wasn't a bug to be fixed—it was her entire operating system.

We calculated relocated charts to see how her stellium moved through different houses. In New York, it fell in her 7th house—all that intensity focused on partnerships. Overwhelming. In Los Angeles, her 10th house—that power channeled into career and public life. Terrifying but potentially brilliant. She chose LA. Five years later, she's running a transformational therapy practice that only takes the most committed clients. Her 'too intense' became her professional superpower because she found where to direct it.

A stellium occurs when three or more planets cluster in the same sign or house, creating concentrated energy in a specific life area or archetypal theme. Unlike T-Squares and Grand Trines which involve three planets in geometric relationship, stelliums involve three or more planets gathered close together. When you activate any line involved in your stellium, you potentially activate all the planets in that cluster simultaneously, creating intense focus and power—or overwhelming concentration that dominates experience. This chapter explores how to work with stellium activation strategically.

Understanding Stellium Dynamics

Stelliums create personality intensification. Three or more planets operating in the same sign produce someone who strongly embodies that sign's qualities. A Scorpio stellium creates someone intensely Scorpionic—deep, transformative, powerful, possibly obsessive. A Gemini stellium creates someone intensely Gemini—communicative, curious, versatile, possibly scattered.

The concentration of energy creates both strength and imbalance. Stellium people excel in areas related to their stellium's sign and house. They struggle in areas requiring balance across different elements or modalities. Someone with a Fire sign stellium may have tremendous initiative and enthusiasm but little emotional depth or practical grounding. Someone with a Water sign stellium may have profound emotional intelligence but difficulty with direct action or logical analysis.

Stelliums function like amplifiers. Whatever themes the sign and house represent become central to identity and life experience. The person returns to these themes repeatedly, working with them from different angles through the various planets in the stellium. Each planet adds nuance while strengthening the overall concentration.

Sign-Based vs House-Based Stelliums

Sign-Based Stelliums

Sign-based stelliums occur when three or more planets occupy the same zodiac sign regardless of house positions. These stelliums emphasize archetypal quality and elemental nature. A Capricorn stellium person embodies Capricornian themes—ambition, discipline, structure, achievement—regardless of which houses the planets occupy.

Sign-based stelliums remain consistent across all locations. Your natal Libra stellium stays in Libra whether you're in New York or Tokyo. The archetypal emphasis doesn't change geographically. However, different locations place the stellium in different houses through relocation, changing which life areas receive the concentrated energy.

House-Based Stelliums

House-based stelliums occur when three or more planets cluster in the same house regardless of zodiac signs. These stelliums emphasize life area and concrete manifestation. A 10th house stellium person focuses intensely on career, reputation, and public life regardless of which signs the planets occupy.

House-based stelliums change with relocation. Your natal 7th house stellium might move to the 9th house in a different city, shifting concentration from partnerships to philosophy, travel, and higher education. This geographical sensitivity makes house-based stellium analysis crucial for relocation planning.

Activating Stellium Lines in Astrocartography

When you travel to a line connected to any planet in your stellium, you activate that planet—but stellium planets don't exist in isolation. The clustered energy means activating one planet often triggers the entire group. The intensity multiplies beyond what single planetary line interpretation would suggest.

Example: Maria's Stellium Activation

Maria has Sun, Mercury, Venus, and Mars in Virgo in her natal 12th house. When she relocated to her Sun line, expecting typical Sun line experiences (confidence, visibility, life purpose), she got those themes but filtered through all four Virgo planets simultaneously. Her confidence (Sun) required analytical precision (Mercury), aesthetic refinement (Venus), and disciplined action (Mars)—all expressed through service and behind-the-scenes work (12th house).

The experience felt overwhelming initially. Four planets demanding expression creates internal pressure even when the demands align thematically. Maria needed time to integrate how to be confidently herself (Sun) while communicating precisely (Mercury), relating beautifully (Venus), and acting efficiently (Mars) all in Virgoan ways. The stellium concentration intensified the Sun line beyond standard interpretation.

Strategic Principle

Choose stellium line locations when you're ready to work intensively with those themes and have support for integration. Avoid stellium lines when you need balance, diversity of experience, or relief from your dominant pattern. Stellium activation amplifies what's already concentrated—beneficial when that serves growth, overwhelming when you need different energies.

Stelliums by Element
Fire Stelliums (Aries, Leo, Sagittarius)

Fire stelliums create passionate, action-oriented, enthusiastic people who struggle with patience and reflection. Three or more Fire planets produce someone who lives through initiative, creativity, and bold expression. On Fire stellium lines, this energy intensifies—tremendous creative output and leadership but potential burnout and scattered focus.

Strategic approach: Use Fire stellium lines for creative projects, leadership roles, and inspiring others. Build in rest periods and reflective practices. Fire stellium people need Water element (emotional depth, quiet reflection) and Earth element (practical grounding, sustainable pace) to balance their natural fire. Choose locations with contemplative environments or slower rhythms that temper intensity.

Earth Stelliums (Taurus, Virgo, Capricorn)

Earth stelliums create practical, grounded, achievement-focused people who struggle with spontaneity and risk. Three or more Earth planets produce someone who lives through building, organizing, and manifesting tangibly. On Earth stellium lines, material success flows naturally but excessive focus on security and practicality can create rigidity.

Strategic approach: Use Earth stellium lines for building businesses, acquiring property, and establishing material foundations. Incorporate Fire element (vision, inspiration) and Air element (mental flexibility, social connection) to prevent excessive materialism. Choose locations with vibrant cultural scenes or innovative communities that add meaning to practical achievement.

Air Stelliums (Gemini, Libra, Aquarius)

Air stelliums create intellectual, communicative, socially adept people who struggle with emotional depth and physical embodiment.

Three or more Air planets produce someone who lives through ideas, communication, and social networks. On Air stellium lines, mental brilliance flourishes but disconnection from feelings and body intensifies.

Strategic approach: Use Air stellium lines for writing, teaching, networking, and intellectual work. Establish embodied practices (yoga, dance, martial arts) and emotional depth work (therapy, intimate relationships) to balance mental focus. Choose locations that emphasize physical beauty, natural environments, or emotional community to ground the Air energy.

Water Stelliums (Cancer, Scorpio, Pisces)

Water stelliums create emotionally deep, intuitive, spiritually sensitive people who struggle with boundaries and practical action. Three or more Water planets produce someone who lives through feeling, imagination, and psychic connection. On Water stellium lines, emotional and spiritual capacities deepen but overwhelming sensitivity and escapism can create dysfunction.

Strategic approach: Use Water stellium lines for healing work, creative arts, and spiritual development. Implement strong boundaries, practical structures, and clear direction to channel depth productively. Choose locations with established spiritual communities, therapeutic resources, or structured creative programs that provide containers for emotional intensity.

House Stelliums and Relocation Strategy

House stelliums shift with relocation, creating different life focus in different locations. Understanding how your stellium moves through houses as you move geographically reveals where your concentrated energy serves you best.

Example: Thomas's Relocating Stellium

Thomas has Sun, Mercury, Venus, and Jupiter in Gemini. In his birthplace (New York), this stellium falls in the 3rd house—communication, local environment, siblings, daily life. His natural Gemini talents (communication, versatility, curiosity) expressed through 3rd house themes. He worked in local media, maintained close sibling relationships, and thrived in his neighborhood community.

When Thomas relocated to Los Angeles, his Gemini stellium moved to the 1st house—identity, appearance, personal initiative. The same planets now expressed through self-presentation and personal brand rather than local communication. He became a public speaker and built a personal media platform. His identity itself became communicative and versatile rather than just his daily activities.

Later, Thomas tried living in London where his Gemini stellium fell in the 9th house—higher education, philosophy, international matters. He began teaching internationally and writing books synthesizing diverse philosophical traditions. The same stellium created entirely different life experiences based solely on house position through relocation.

Strategic Relocation Principle

Calculate relocated charts for any serious relocation candidates to see which houses receive your stellium. Match stellium house placement to current life goals. If you need career focus, relocate where your stellium falls in the 10th house. If you need relationship development, choose locations placing your stellium in the 7th house. Your stellium's concentration becomes strategic asset when geographically directed toward relevant life areas.

Transits to Stelliums

Stelliums create concentrated intensity. Four planets activating simultaneously is powerful but can be overwhelming. Jupiter transiting your four-planet Capricorn stellium brings expansion and opportunity but across four planetary areas at once—career growth, structural changes, authority increases, and ambitious goals all expanding simultaneously. Without strategic planning, even beneficial transits create overwhelm through sheer volume.

Transit Timing Guidelines

- Slow-moving planet conjunctions to stelliums: Major life chapter activations lasting years, fundamentally restructuring stellium themes
- Saturn transiting stellium: Maturation and discipline across all stellium areas, potentially exhausting but strengthening
- Jupiter transiting stellium: Expansion and opportunity overload, requires prioritization and boundaries
- Uranus transiting stellium: Revolutionary breakthrough or destabilizing chaos across all stellium areas
- Neptune transiting stellium: Spiritual opening or confusing dissolution of structures, extreme sensitivity
- Pluto transiting stellium: Complete transformation through death-rebirth, often crisis-catalyzed

Avoid relocating to stellium lines during multiple challenging outer planet transits to the stellium. One challenging transit creates growth opportunity; three simultaneous challenging transits creates crisis. Plan stellium line relocations during supportive transits or periods when only one major transit is active.

Balancing Stellium Concentration

Stellium people benefit from conscious balance work. The concentration creates strength but also blind spots. Someone with a strong Scorpio stellium may have profound psychological insight but lack Taurus grounding and sensual presence. Someone with a strong Sagittarius stellium may have inspiring vision but lack Gemini attention to detail and local connection.

Balancing Strategies

Identify your stellium's opposite sign (polarity partner). A Taurus stellium needs Scorpio depth; a Scorpio stellium needs Taurus simplicity. Consciously develop opposite sign qualities through practices, relationships, or location choices. Travel to lines connected to planets in your stellium's opposite element for balance experiences.

Seek relationships with people strong in elements or modalities you lack. Your Water stellium benefits from partnership with strong Fire or Earth people who provide what you naturally miss. Your Cardinal stellium benefits from Fixed people who provide stability and persistence.

Use stellium lines for intensive periods of focused work, but alternate with locations that activate different chart areas. Three years on your stellium line building expertise followed by two years on lines that develop other life areas creates sustainable growth rather than imbalanced specialization.

Professional Guidance for Stellium Consultations

When clients have stelliums, help them understand both the gifts and the imbalances. Stellium people often identify so strongly with their concentration that they can't see what they're missing. Your outside perspective provides valuable reality checking and balance suggestions.

Calculate relocated charts showing different house placements for the stellium. Visual demonstration of how the same planets create different life experiences geographically helps clients make informed choices. Point out which locations place the stellium in houses aligned with current goals and which create unwanted emphasis.

Track upcoming transits to clients' stelliums carefully. Outer planet transits to stelliums create major life chapters that benefit from advance preparation. When Pluto begins transiting a four-planet stellium, the person needs to know years in advance to prepare psychologically, financially, and structurally for transformation.

Help stellium clients recognize when their concentration becomes liability. Someone with a 12th house stellium may excel at spiritual work but struggle with practical visibility and material success. Recommending locations that move the stellium to the 10th house for career development periods provides strategic relief from dominant pattern while still honoring stellium strengths.

Multi-Planet Stelliums (4+ Planets)

Stelliums of four or more planets create extreme concentration. These people often feel like walking embodiments of a single sign or house theme. The intensity can produce genius-level mastery or overwhelming imbalance depending on consciousness and support.

Working with Large Stelliums

Accept that you'll never achieve perfect balance—your concentration is your destiny and your gift. Rather than trying to become well-rounded, develop extraordinary mastery in stellium areas while maintaining minimum competence in other areas. Use your concentration strategically rather than fighting against it.

Build support teams that complement your stellium. If you have a five-planet Virgo stellium making you brilliant at analysis and service but terrible at self-promotion, hire marketing help. If you have a five-planet Leo stellium making you charismatic and creative but disorganized, hire administrative support. Professional success with major stelliums often requires acknowledging limitations and compensating through collaboration.

Consider living on stellium lines only during specific life phases when intensive focus serves clear goals. Spend young adulthood developing stellium mastery, middle years balancing with other chart areas, later years integrating stellium wisdom into broader life perspective.

Strategic timing prevents stellium concentration from dominating entire life trajectory.

Stelliums represent astrocartography's concentrated power. These configurations create focused intensity that can manifest as genius or imbalance, extraordinary achievement or narrow limitation. With conscious understanding, strategic activation, and willingness to balance concentration with diversity, stellium lines become platforms for developing rare excellence while maintaining sustainable life structures. The concentration is real and powerful—what you do with that concentrated energy, where you direct it geographically, and how you balance it with complementary experiences determines whether stelliums become gifts or curses.

Chapter Thirteen

Transit Timing: When to Activate Which Lines

My client Jessica called me in tears. She'd been planning her move to Barcelona for six months—she'd found the perfect apartment, negotiated remote work with her company, even started learning Spanish. Her Venus Descendant line ran right through the city, and she'd been dreaming of the relationship possibilities. But something kept stopping her from buying the plane ticket. Every time she tried to book it, she felt this knot in her stomach she couldn't explain.

When we looked at her chart together, everything became clear. Yes, Venus on the Descendant promised relationship activation. But her natal Venus squared Saturn—a tight 2-degree aspect I'd noted in her chart analysis. And Saturn was currently opposing her Venus from across the sky, activating that natal square geographically. The knot in her stomach wasn't fear or cold feet. It was her chart speaking. Her Venus-Saturn square was saying 'not yet.'

We looked six months ahead. Jupiter would be trining her natal Venus then—activating both the Venus-Saturn square and that aspect's inherent challenges, but also bringing Jupiter's grace and timing to soften the restriction. 'What if you go then instead?' I suggested. Her whole body relaxed. 'That feels right,' she said. 'I don't know why, but it does.'

She went to Barcelona during the Jupiter transit. She met someone within two weeks. The relationship had its Venus-Saturn themes—there was a significant age gap, and they had to work through commitment fears—but the Jupiter trine provided exactly enough optimism and faith to work through the challenges. They're still together three years later. Same city, same Venus line—but completely different experience because of timing.

This is what understanding transits does for your astrocartography practice. It transforms your static map into a living, breathing strategic tool. When Jupiter transits your natal Sun, that transit simultaneously activates every planet that aspects your Sun. When you're on lines connected to your Sun's aspect web, the activation intensifies geographically. This chapter provides planet-by-planet guidance for timing relocations and travels based on which transits are activating which aspect patterns.

Each transiting planet operates on its own timeline and carries distinct energy. Fast-moving planets (Moon, Mercury, Venus, Mars) create short-term activations lasting days to months. Slow-moving planets (Jupiter, Saturn, Uranus, Neptune, Pluto) create sustained activations lasting months to years. Strategic timing requires understanding both the transit's nature and your natal aspect web's structure.

Solar Transits: Annual Cycle of Identity and Purpose

The Sun completes its zodiac cycle annually, transiting each natal planet once per year. Solar transits activate identity, vitality, and life purpose themes. When the Sun transits a natal planet, it illuminates that planetary energy and every planet aspecting it.

Duration

The Sun spends approximately one month in each zodiac sign, creating month-long windows when specific natal planets receive solar activation. The exact transit (Sun conjunct, square, trine, or opposite natal planet) lasts 2-3 days with a 1-degree orb, though the surrounding weeks carry related energy.

Strategic Application

Plan short trips during solar transits to natal planets involved in important aspect webs. If your natal Mars trines Jupiter and squares Saturn, when the Sun transits Mars, travel to Mars line locations for 2-3 days of concentrated activation. Solar transits work well for testing lines before committing to longer stays. The activation is brief but clarifying—you experience the line's essential quality without sustained pressure.

Example: James has Venus trine Neptune and Venus square Pluto. Each year when the Sun transits his natal Venus (late Taurus), he experiences intensified romantic and creative themes. Traveling to his Venus line during this window amplifies the annual Venus activation geographically. The Sun illuminates both the trine's spiritual romance potential and the square's intensity. The 2-3 day trip provides concentrated insight into how his Venus web functions in that location.

Lunar Transits: Monthly Emotional Rhythm

The Moon completes its zodiac cycle in approximately 28 days, transiting each natal planet monthly. Lunar transits activate emotional responses, subconscious patterns, and immediate needs. Moon transits are the fastest, most frequent activations in astrology.

Duration

The Moon spends approximately 2.5 days in each sign, creating brief activations. The exact Moon-to-natal-planet aspect lasts hours, though emotional effects may linger for the full 2.5-day period while Moon transits that sign.

Strategic Application

Lunar transits work best for daily timing rather than relocation planning. However, lunar return charts (calculated when transiting Moon returns to natal Moon position monthly) reveal optimal short-trip timing. If you're planning a weekend visit to test a line, time it during supportive lunar transits to planets involved in that line's aspect web.

Track void-of-course Moon periods—when Moon makes its final aspect in a sign before changing signs. Avoid initiating important relocations or signing leases during void Moon. The lack of aspectual connection creates ungroundedness that manifests as forgotten details or unexpected complications.

Mercury Transits: Communication and Connection Cycles

Mercury completes its zodiac cycle in approximately one year, spending 2-3 weeks in each sign typically. Mercury retrograde periods (three times yearly for about three weeks each) extend stays in specific signs. Mercury transits activate communication, travel, contracts, and local environment themes.

Duration

Mercury typically transits each natal planet once yearly, though retrograde motion can create three passes (direct, retrograde, direct again) over several months. Exact Mercury-to-natal-planet aspects last 1-3 days depending on Mercury's speed.

Strategic Application

Mercury transits excel for short trips and location research. When Mercury transits natal planets connected to lines you're considering, visit for reconnaissance. The mental clarity and communication activation help you gather information and assess fit. Avoid signing leases or contracts during Mercury retrograde, especially on Mercury lines or when Mercury retrogrades over planets aspecting your Mercury.

Example: Rachel has Mercury trine Saturn and Mercury square Uranus. When transiting Mercury aspects her natal Mercury, she visits her Mercury line cities. During the trine activation, communication flows naturally and she gathers reliable information. The square activation brings unexpected insights but also technological glitches and communication mishaps. She avoids Mercury retrograde periods for serious Mercury line business.

Venus Transits: Love, Beauty, and Value Cycles

Venus completes its zodiac cycle in approximately one year, spending 3-5 weeks in each sign typically. Venus retrograde (every 18 months for about six weeks) extends stays and creates review periods. Venus transits activate relationship, pleasure, aesthetic, and financial themes.

Duration

Venus transits each natal planet once yearly in normal years, though retrograde can create extended activations or multiple passes. Exact Venus-to-natal-planet aspects last 2-4 days depending on Venus's speed.

Strategic Application

Venus transits provide optimal timing for relationship-focused travel and creative projects on Venus lines. When Venus transits natal planets aspecting your Venus, romantic and creative energy flows toward those planetary themes. Avoid beginning serious relationships or making major financial commitments during Venus retrograde, especially on Venus lines. Use retrograde periods for reassessing values and relationship patterns.

If your natal Venus squares Pluto, when transiting Venus aspects Venus or Pluto, intensity in relationships amplifies. On Venus lines during these transits, obsessive attraction patterns surface clearly. This awareness allows conscious choice rather than unconscious compulsion.

Mars Transits: Action, Assertion, and Energy Cycles

Mars completes its zodiac cycle in approximately two years, spending 6-7 weeks in each sign typically. Mars retrograde (every two years for 2-3 months) extends stays and redirects action. Mars transits activate drive, assertion, sexuality, and conflict themes.

Duration

Mars transits each natal planet roughly every two years. Retrograde motion can create three passes lasting several months. Exact Mars-to-natal-planet aspects last 3-5 days, though the surrounding weeks carry related energy due to Mars's relatively slow movement.

Strategic Application

Mars transits provide power for initiating action on Mars lines and any lines connected to planets aspecting natal Mars. When Mars transits your natal Mars, Mars line energy peaks—excellent for competitive activities, launching ventures, or physical challenges. Avoid Mars retrograde periods for beginning aggressive new projects on Mars lines. Use retrograde for strategy revision and building strength without competing.

Example: Michael has Mars trine Sun and Mars square Moon. When transiting Mars aspects his natal Mars, he visits Mars line locations. The Sun trine activation brings confident action aligned with identity. The Moon square activation creates emotional friction requiring conscious management. He schedules athletic competitions during trine periods and practices during square periods.

Jupiter Transits: Expansion, Growth, and Opportunity

Jupiter completes its zodiac cycle in approximately 12 years, spending roughly one year in each sign. Jupiter retrograde (annually for about four months) creates review periods. Jupiter transits activate expansion, optimism, meaning, and growth themes.

Duration

Jupiter transits each natal planet once every 12 years, though retrograde can create three passes over several months. The exact aspect lasts several days to a week, though Jupiter's influence extends for weeks before and after exactness.

Strategic Application

Jupiter transits provide optimal windows for major relocations to Jupiter lines and lines connected to planets aspecting natal Jupiter. The year-long stay in each sign creates sustained expansion opportunity. When Jupiter transits natal planets in your aspect web, those planetary themes experience growth, opportunity, and increased visibility.

Plan significant moves during Jupiter transits rather than fighting against challenging transits. If your natal Jupiter trines Venus and squares Saturn, when transiting Jupiter aspects natal Jupiter, Venus receives harmonious expansion while Saturn demands realistic planning. Jupiter lines during this period support optimistic growth tempered by mature responsibility.

Jupiter retrograde periods benefit internal growth more than external expansion. Use retrograde for ensuring recent growth is sustainable and meaningful rather than pursuing more opportunity. On Jupiter lines during retrograde, consolidate rather than expand.

Saturn Transits: Structure, Discipline, and Maturation

Saturn completes its zodiac cycle in approximately 29.5 years, spending 2.5-3 years in each sign. Saturn retrograde (annually for 4-5 months) creates review periods. Saturn transits activate responsibility, limitation, discipline, and maturation themes.

Duration

Saturn transits each natal planet once every 29 years, though retrograde can create three passes over a year or more. Saturn's slow movement means exact aspects can remain active for weeks, and the surrounding months carry heavy Saturnian influence.

Strategic Application

Saturn transits demand realistic assessment before relocating to Saturn lines or lines connected to planets aspecting natal Saturn. These multi-year periods bring maturation through challenge, restriction, and necessary discipline. Only relocate to Saturn-connected lines during Saturn transits if you're genuinely ready for intensive growth work.

The Saturn return (age 28-30, 57-60) intensifies all Saturn line experiences dramatically. Many people naturally relocate during Saturn returns to establish adult foundations. If considering Saturn line relocation during your return, ensure extraordinary support systems and realistic expectations.

Saturn retrograde periods benefit reassessing structures rather than building new ones. On Saturn lines during retrograde, question whether current commitments serve authentic goals or stem from obligation and fear.

Uranus Transits: Revolution, Awakening, and Liberation

Uranus completes its zodiac cycle in approximately 84 years, spending about 7 years in each sign. Uranus retrograde (annually for about 5 months) internalizes revolutionary energy. Uranus transits activate breakthrough, disruption, awakening, and liberation themes.

Duration

Uranus transits each natal planet once in a lifetime or never, depending on lifespan. Retrograde motion creates multiple passes lasting a year or more. The exact aspect activates for weeks, but the entire transit period spanning years carries Uranian themes.

Strategic Application

Uranus transits to natal planets create 1-2 year windows for experimental relocation to Uranus lines or lines connected to aspected planets. These periods support breaking free from restrictions and trying unconventional approaches. The revolutionary energy either catalyzes brilliant breakthrough or creates chaotic disruption—preparation and support systems determine which.

Uranus transits work well for temporary relocations and trials rather than permanent moves. The unpredictable nature means circumstances may change suddenly. If your natal Uranus squares Mercury, when transiting Uranus aspects Uranus or Mercury, communication and thinking become brilliantly innovative or frantically scattered. Test Uranus-connected lines during these periods rather than committing blindly.

Neptune Transits: Dissolution, Spirituality, and Transcendence

Neptune completes its zodiac cycle in approximately 165 years, spending about 14 years in each sign. Neptune retrograde (annually for about 5 months) deepens spiritual reflection. Neptune transits activate mysticism, dissolution, compassion, and confusion themes.

Duration

Neptune transits each natal planet once in a lifetime if at all. Retrograde creates multiple passes over 2-3 years. The extended timeframe means entire life chapters unfold under Neptune's influence.

Strategic Application

Neptune transits require extraordinary discernment for relocation decisions. The boundary dissolution can create spiritual awakening or complete delusion. Relocating to Neptune lines during Neptune transits intensifies both transcendent potential and risk of escapism or deception. Ensure therapeutic support and grounded friends who provide reality checks.

Neptune transits to natal planets aspecting Neptune multiply the dissolution effect. If your natal Neptune squares Venus, when transiting Neptune aspects Neptune or Venus, romantic illusion peaks. Neptune line travel during this period requires conscious awareness of projection and fantasy. Creative and spiritual work thrives; practical decision-making suffers.

Pluto Transits: Transformation, Power, and Rebirth

Pluto completes its zodiac cycle in approximately 248 years, spending 12-30 years in each sign depending on orbit eccentricity. Pluto retrograde (annually for about 5 months) intensifies internal transformation. Pluto transits activate death-rebirth, power, obsession, and evolution themes.

Duration

Pluto transits each natal planet once in a lifetime at most. Retrograde creates multiple passes over several years. The transformation unfolds gradually across extended timeframes, fundamentally restructuring personality and life circumstances.

Strategic Application

Pluto transits represent the most intense, transformative timing for working with Pluto lines or lines connected to planets aspecting natal Pluto. Only relocate during Pluto transits if genuinely prepared for complete life restructuring. The process destroys what no longer serves to make space for authentic power and purpose.

Pluto transits to natal planets in aspect webs create years-long initiations. If your natal Pluto trines Sun and squares Moon, when transiting Pluto aspects Pluto, your entire identity-emotion structure undergoes transformation. Pluto line relocation during this transit accelerates and intensifies the process—empowering for those ready, overwhelming for those unprepared.

Support systems become essential during Pluto transits. Therapy, spiritual practice, and trusted guides help navigate the underworld journey. Pluto transits on Pluto-connected lines can catalyze profound healing and empowerment when approached consciously with adequate resources.

Nodal Transits: Karmic Timing and Evolutionary Windows

The North and South Nodes move retrograde through the zodiac, completing the cycle in approximately 18.6 years. Nodal transits activate destiny, karma, and evolutionary direction themes.

Duration

The nodes spend about 18 months in each sign. Nodal returns (when transiting nodes return to natal positions) occur around ages 18-19, 37-38, 56-57, 75-76, marking major evolutionary chapters.

Strategic Application

Nodal transits to natal planets involved in aspect webs create powerful timing for soul-level relocation. When transiting North Node aspects natal planets, those themes support evolutionary growth. When transiting South Node aspects natal planets, those themes involve releasing past patterns.

During nodal returns, relocating to nodal lines intensifies karmic themes dramatically. These 18.6-year cycles mark natural life transitions when major location changes serve soul evolution. The nodal return creates a portal—use it consciously.

Chiron Transits: Healing Cycles and Wisdom Integration

Chiron completes its zodiac cycle in approximately 50 years, spending 1-8 years in each sign (highly variable orbit). The Chiron return around age 50 marks profound healing and teaching integration.

Strategic Application

Chiron transits to natal planets create optimal windows for healing work on Chiron lines or lines connected to planets aspecting natal Chiron. The wounding becomes medicine when approached consciously. Therapeutic support amplifies benefits during these periods.

The Chiron return (ages 48-51) represents the most powerful timing for Chiron line work. The lifetime of wounding-healing reaches integration. Many people transition into teaching or healing professions during Chiron return. Relocating to Chiron lines during this period can catalyze profound life purpose realization.

Synthesizing Multiple Transits for Strategic Timing

Real-world timing involves multiple simultaneous transits. Strategic relocation considers the entire transit picture rather than isolated planetary movements. When Saturn trines your natal Sun while Jupiter squares your natal Moon, moving to Sun line locations brings both disciplined identity strengthening and emotional expansion challenges.

Create transit timelines for major relocations. Map all significant transits for the 6-12 months surrounding potential move dates. Look for periods when supportive transits outnumber challenging ones, or when challenging transits activate aspect webs you're prepared to work with consciously.

Remember that difficult transits aren't obstacles when you're ready for the growth they catalyze. Saturn square natal Venus on Venus lines forces relationship maturation—exhausting for someone seeking easy romance, transformative for someone committed to authentic partnership. Know yourself, know the timing, choose consciously.

Transit tracking becomes ongoing practice rather than one-time planning. Regular review of upcoming transits allows adjusting location strategy as cosmic weather changes. The integration of natal aspects, geographic activation, and transit timing creates the most sophisticated astrocartography practice possible.

Chapter Fourteen

Real-World Case Studies: Theory Meets Practice

Last month, three different clients emailed me the exact same question: 'I understand the theory. But what do I actually DO with all this information when I need to make a real decision?' They'd all read books, studied their charts, mapped their aspect webs. They understood natal aspects, transits, configurations. But when it came time to actually choose between San Francisco and Seattle, or decide whether to take that job in Austin, they froze.

I get it. Theory is clean. Real life is messy. In theory, you carefully evaluate natal aspects, check upcoming transits, synthesize patterns, and make the optimal choice. In reality, you have a job offer that expires in two weeks, a relationship pulling you one direction, family obligations pulling another, and a gut feeling that may or may not be fear masquerading as intuition.

So I started collecting case studies. Real clients, real decisions, real outcomes. Not the 'perfect' scenarios where everything aligns beautifully, but the complicated ones where you have to weigh competing factors and make the best choice with imperfect information. These are the scenarios that taught me more than any textbook ever could. Theory becomes practical through application. This chapter presents ten real-world decision-making scenarios showing how to use the aspect web framework in actual situations. Each scenario includes the question, relevant natal aspects, upcoming transits, analysis, and recommended decision with reasoning.

Scenario One: Career Relocation

Question

Sarah received a job offer in Austin on her Mars Midheaven line. Should she accept? She's 31, single, ready for career advancement but concerned about work-life balance.

Natal Aspects

Mars at 22 degrees Leo trines Sun at 19 degrees Aries (3-degree orb) and squares Saturn at 21 degrees Taurus (1-degree orb). Mixed aspects, one flowing and one challenging, both tight.

Upcoming Transits

Jupiter will trine her Mars in eight months. Saturn will square her Mars in fourteen months, activating the natal Mars-Saturn square.

Analysis

Mars Midheaven activates career drive and public achievement. The Mars-Sun trine provides confidence and energy that supports professional success. The Mars-Saturn square creates tension between ambition and limitation, between pushing forward and holding back.

The Jupiter trine in eight months will amplify both Mars drive and the Sun trine, creating exceptional career opportunities. The Saturn square in fourteen months will test sustainability and demand mature management of Mars energy. Her concern about work-life balance aligns with the Mars-Saturn square warning.

Recommendation

Accept the position but negotiate clear boundaries around work hours from the start. The Mars-Saturn square will demand this eventually. Better to establish boundaries proactively than reactively. Plan for maximum career push during the Jupiter trine period (first year), then consciously pull back when Saturn squares Mars to prevent burnout. The Mars-Sun trine ensures she has natural energy for the work. The challenge is managing the Mars-Saturn tension between drive and discipline.

Scenario Two: Relationship Decision

Question

Michael met someone special while traveling. She lives in Paris on his Venus Descendant line. Should he relocate for the relationship? He's 38, divorced, cautious about commitment.

Natal Aspects

Venus at 18 degrees Libra squares Pluto at 17 degrees Capricorn (1-degree orb) and trines Jupiter at 16 degrees Gemini (2-degree orb). One challenging and one harmonious aspect, both very tight.

Upcoming Transits

Pluto will square his Venus from Aquarius next year, activating the natal Venus-Pluto square. No other major transits to Venus for two years.

Analysis

Venus Descendant activates partnership focus. The Venus-Pluto square brings intensity, power dynamics, and transformation through relationship. Given his divorce history and caution about commitment, this aspect likely played a role in past relationship challenges. The Venus-Jupiter trine provides optimism and generosity that softens Plutonian intensity. The upcoming Pluto square to Venus will intensify an already intense natal pattern. This is not light, easy relationship energy. This is deep transformation work through partnership.

Recommendation

Don't relocate immediately. Visit extended periods first. The Venus-Pluto square means Paris relationships will be intense, possibly obsessive or controlling. His caution is natal wisdom speaking. The Pluto transit next year will test the relationship severely. Better to test the connection through visits before full relocation commitment. If the relationship survives the Pluto transit while he's visiting rather than living there, then consider permanent relocation. The Venus-Jupiter trine ensures some ease, but the double Pluto activation (natal square plus transit) requires exceptional consciousness and possibly therapy support.

Scenario Three: Recovery Location

Question

After burnout and health crisis, Jennifer needs a recovery location for six months. She's considering Sedona on her Moon IC line or Santa Fe on her Jupiter IC line.

Natal Aspects

Moon at 21 degrees Cancer trines Venus at 22 degrees Pisces and Neptune at 6 degrees Scorpio, forming Water Grand Trine. Jupiter at 8 degrees Sagittarius squares Sun at 8 degrees Virgo and opposes Saturn at 13 degrees Gemini, forming a mutable T-Square with Jupiter at apex.

Upcoming Transits

Saturn will trine her Moon in four months. No major transits to Jupiter for eighteen months.

Analysis

Moon IC with Grand Trine in water provides maximum emotional ease, intuitive flow, and gentle recovery conditions. This is ideal for healing. Jupiter IC with T-Square at apex provides expansion but also pressure. Jupiter apex means constant demand for optimism and growth even when she needs rest. After burnout, T-Square activation is contraindicated. The Grand Trine provides exactly what recovery requires: ease, flow, and natural support.

Recommendation

Choose Sedona (Moon IC with Grand Trine). This is not the time for Jupiter's expansion pressure. She needs Moon's nurturing and the Grand Trine's effortless flow. The Saturn trine to Moon in four months will provide gentle structure without pressure, helping her establish sustainable recovery practices. After six months when she's restored, she can revisit Jupiter line for expansion. Right now, ease trumps growth.

Scenario Four: Stellium Timing

Question

David has Sun, Mercury, Venus, and Mars all in Aries between 22-18 degrees. His stellium lines run through Austin. He's considering moving there to launch his business. When should he go?

Upcoming Transits

Jupiter will transit Aries crossing all stellium planets in ten months. Saturn will transit Aries crossing all stellium planets in three years.

Analysis

Stelliums create concentrated intensity. Four planets activating simultaneously is powerful but can be overwhelming. Jupiter transiting the stellium creates maximum expansion opportunity. Every planet gets Jupiter's optimism and growth. This is perfect for business launch. Saturn transiting the stellium in three years will test everything built during Jupiter period, demanding sustainability and maturity.

Recommendation

Move to Austin six months before Jupiter enters Aries, giving time to establish basics before maximum expansion hits. Use the Jupiter transit year for aggressive business growth, networking, and market expansion. After Jupiter moves on, scale back intensity before Saturn arrives. Plan to either have the business fully established and sustainable by Saturn's arrival, or plan to relocate before Saturn hits the stellium. Back-to-back stellium transits are exhausting. Strategic timing prevents burnout.

Additional Scenarios Summary

These scenarios demonstrate the decision-making process in action. The pattern is always the same: identify the lines, map the natal aspects, check upcoming transits, evaluate the combinations, and decide based on complete information plus personal readiness. Practice with your own chart and real decisions. The framework becomes intuitive with use. You'll start automatically checking aspects and transits before making any location decisions, transforming astrocartography from interesting theory into practical strategic tool.

Chapter Fifteen

Creating Your Personal Astrocartography Strategy

I remember the exact moment Emma realized she'd actually learned this. We were on a Zoom call, and she'd just pulled up her aspect web document, her transit calendar, and her astrocartography map—all organized, color-coded, ready to use. Six months earlier, she'd been completely overwhelmed, drowning in aspect tables and transit dates, unable to make a single decision without calling me in a panic.

Now she was walking me through her analysis of a potential move to Nashville. 'My Venus line runs through there,' she said, 'and Venus trines my Jupiter natally, so that's supportive. But Saturn's about to square my Venus in eight months, which will activate both the Jupiter trine and create temporary tension. So I'm thinking I'll move there during the Jupiter trine to Venus next month, establish myself while the energy is flowing, and then I'll already be settled when the Saturn square hits.'

I just sat there smiling. She didn't need me anymore. She had the framework. She knew her chart. She understood the timing. The methodology had become intuitive. That's what this final chapter is about—not just teaching you the system, but helping you internalize it so completely that it becomes second nature. Not just knowledge, but wisdom.

You have the complete framework. Now it's time to create your personal astrocartography strategy, a living document that guides your location decisions for years to come. This final chapter provides worksheets, action steps, and ongoing practices for integrating aspect web awareness into your life planning.

Creating Your Personal Timing Calendar

Get a calendar or spreadsheet covering the next five years. Mark every major transit to planets in your chart that have significant aspects. Use different colors for different planets. Red for Saturn transits, blue for Jupiter, purple for outer planets. This visual timeline shows when major activations occur, helping you plan travel and relocation strategically around beneficial or challenging periods.

For each marked transit, note which natal aspects that transit will activate. Saturn crossing your Venus? Note that it activates Venus-Jupiter trine, Venus-Saturn square, and Venus-Mars sextile. You instantly see the complexity of that period. Mark whether the overall pattern is supportive, challenging, or mixed. This calendar becomes your strategic planning tool.

Best Lines for You Based on Your Aspects

Review your complete aspect web from Chapter 2. Identify which planets have predominantly harmonious aspects (multiple trines and sextiles, few or no squares and oppositions). These are your naturally supportive lines, your safe harbors and power zones. You can travel to these lines almost any time and expect relative ease and natural advantage.

Identify which planets have predominantly challenging aspects (multiple squares and oppositions, few or no trines and sextiles).

These are your growth-work lines, locations that will demand effort and consciousness but provide profound development when you're ready. Plan to visit these lines during supportive transit periods and when you have strong support systems in place.

Identify which planets have mixed aspects, both harmonious and challenging in roughly equal measure. These are your complex lines, requiring nuanced navigation and conscious choice about when and how to engage them. The harmonious aspects provide resources for working with challenges, but you need to consciously activate those resources.

Lines to Use with Caution

Some lines require extra care based on your natal aspects. If you have natal Sun square Saturn and that square has caused depression, restriction, or low self-worth throughout your life, Sun lines during Saturn transits are high-risk. Not forbidden, but requiring exceptional consciousness and support. Mark these combinations in your calendar with warning flags.

If you have natal Venus-Pluto challenging aspects and history of obsessive or destructive relationships, Venus lines during Pluto transits require therapy support and strong boundaries. Again, not forbidden, but definitely not casual vacation destinations without preparation. Know your vulnerable combinations and treat them with appropriate respect.

Optimal Timing for Major Lines

For each major line you're interested in, calculate optimal timing windows. When do harmonious transits cross that line's planet? When do challenging transits hit? If you're considering Paris on your Venus line and Jupiter will trine your Venus in two years while Pluto squares it in four years, the obvious optimal window is during the Jupiter trine. Book your Paris trip or relocation for that period.

Sometimes the optimal window is now, simply because no major difficult transits are approaching. If your Moon line has harmonious natal aspects and no challenging transits for three years, any time in that window works well. Don't wait for perfection. Work with available good-enough timing when that's what's present.

Action Steps and Worksheets

Action Step One: Complete Your Aspect Web Document

If you haven't already, create the complete aspect web document from Chapter 2. List every planet with all its aspects, organized clearly. This is your permanent reference. Update it if you discover aspects you missed initially. Keep it accessible for quick consultation when making decisions.

Action Step Two: Create Your Five-Year Transit Calendar

Mark every major transit to aspected planets. Color-code by planet. Note which aspects each transit activates. This takes several hours initially but saves countless hours of confusion and poor timing later. Update annually as new transit information becomes available.

Action Step Three: Identify Your Top Five Lines

Based on your natal aspects, life goals, and current needs, identify the five planetary lines most relevant for you right now. Research cities and regions on those lines. Note upcoming transit timing for those lines. This creates a focused target list rather than overwhelming yourself with too many options.

Action Step Four: Plan Your Next Trip or Relocation

Using the decision matrix from Chapter 12, evaluate your next planned trip or relocation through the aspect web lens. Go through all five steps. Make your decision based on complete information rather than guessing or hoping. Document your decision-making process so you can learn from the results.

Action Step Five: Track Your Experiences

Keep a location journal. After traveling to any line, write about your experience. Which aspects manifested? How did transits affect the activation? What surprised you? What confirmed your predictions? This tracking builds your personal database of how your unique aspect web manifests geographically. You become your own expert on your chart.

Ongoing Practice and Refinement

Aspect web astrocartography is not a one-time analysis. It's an ongoing practice of integrating natal patterns, current transits, and geographic activation into strategic life planning. Review your aspect web and transit calendar quarterly. Update your top five lines list as your life circumstances and goals evolve. Refine your understanding based on actual experiences rather than just theory.

The sophistication you've developed through this book places you in the top tier of astrocartography practitioners. Most people working with locational astrology never learn about aspect activation. You now have access to the hidden variable that determines actual experience. Use this knowledge responsibly, generously, and consciously. Let it guide you toward locations and timing that support your highest development and deepest fulfillment.

Final Thoughts

Your birth chart is a map of your psyche. Your astrocartography map is that psyche spread across the globe. Your natal aspects are the hidden architecture determining how each geographic activation actually feels and functions. Understanding this three-dimensional integration of chart, aspects, and geography transforms location from random choice or surface preferences into conscious strategic alignment with your soul's journey.

Some locations will call you toward ease and restoration. Other locations will demand growth and transformation. The key is knowing which is which, choosing consciously based on your current readiness, and timing your choices to maximize support and minimize unnecessary suffering. This is the art and science of advanced astrocartography.

May your travels be strategic, your relocations be aligned, and your geographic choices serve your highest becoming. The world is vast, your chart is unique, and the intersection of the two holds infinite possibilities for discovery, development, and fulfillment. Go forth with wisdom, consciousness, and the advantage that understanding your aspect web provides. Your perfect places await.

Conclusion

The Master's Journey

I was teaching a workshop in Milan when a student raised her hand during the Q&A. 'When will I know I've mastered this?' she asked. 'When will I stop second-guessing myself and just know?'

The room went quiet. Everyone wanted the answer. They'd spent three days learning aspect webs, transit timing, configuration analysis—their notebooks were full, their heads were spinning, and they were all thinking the same thing: When does this get easier?

I looked at her and said something that surprised even me: 'You'll never stop second-guessing yourself. Mastery isn't certainty. It's knowing what questions to ask.'

She looked disappointed, so I continued. 'Right now, you're asking "Will this Venus line be good for me?" That's a beginner's question. In six months, you'll be asking "How will my Venus-Saturn square manifest during this Saturn transit on my Venus line, and am I ready for that level of relationship maturation work?" That's a master's question. See the difference?'

Mastery isn't about having all the answers. It's about developing such sophisticated questions that the answers reveal themselves naturally through your understanding of the system. You've spent this entire book learning to ask better questions.

What You've Actually Learned

Let's be honest about what just happened. You didn't just learn some advanced astrology techniques. You learned a completely different way of seeing location, timing, and human development.

You learned that planetary lines aren't fortune cookie predictions but activations of complex natal patterns. That same Venus line means completely different things for someone with Venus trine Jupiter versus Venus square Pluto. The line doesn't change—the natal architecture determines everything.

You learned that timing isn't just about finding "good" transits but about understanding how transits activate your entire aspect web. Saturn crossing your Venus isn't just a Saturn-Venus event—it's the activation of every planet aspecting your natal Venus, creating a cascade of experiences that require sophisticated navigation.

You learned that challenging configurations aren't curses but growth engines requiring consciousness. T-Squares create pressure that forges character. Grand Trines offer ease that can waste potential or develop genius depending on your awareness. Stelliums concentrate energy that manifests as obsession or mastery based on how consciously you direct that focus.

You learned that special points—Chiron, the Nodes, Vertex, Part of Fortune—add layers of meaning that transform surface-level interpretation into soul-level guidance. A Venus line becomes entirely different when Venus aspects your North Node, your Chiron, or your Vertex. The depth reveals itself only when you know where to look.

Most importantly, you learned that astrocartography is never about the map alone. It's always about the person consulting the map, their readiness, their resources, their moment in the great cycles of growth and consolidation that define a life. The same location at different times, with different transits, different levels of support, different degrees of consciousness—completely different experiences.

The Weight of Knowledge

Here's something nobody tells you about mastery: it's heavy. You can't unsee what you now see. You'll look at someone's chart and immediately recognize the challenging patterns they're trying to work through. You'll see the perfect timing windows they're missing. You'll notice when they're on lines that are activating their most difficult aspects without adequate support.

And you won't always be able to help them. They'll want simple answers—"Should I move to Austin or stay in Portland?"—and you'll see a dozen variables that make simple answers impossible. You'll want to explain about their Mars-Saturn square, the upcoming Pluto transit, the T-Square activation, the stellium concentration, but their eyes will glaze over because they just want you to choose for them.

This is the master's burden: seeing complexity that others can't see, understanding nuance that others won't appreciate, holding space for uncertainty when others demand certainty. Sometimes you'll simplify your analysis because the client isn't ready for the full truth. Sometimes you'll watch people make choices you know will be difficult because they're not ready to hear why.

But sometimes—and this makes everything worthwhile—you'll meet someone ready for sophisticated guidance. Someone who can hold the complexity, who wants to understand the deeper patterns, who's prepared to work with challenging transits consciously rather than avoid them. For those people, this level of mastery becomes transformative. You're not just helping them choose a location. You're teaching them to read their own lives with astrological wisdom.

Mastery as Ongoing Practice

If you're waiting for the day when astrocartography analysis becomes automatic, when you can just glance at a chart and know everything instantly, I have disappointing news: that day never comes. Every chart reveals something new. Every client situation presents unique variables. Every location decision requires fresh thinking.

What does develop is pattern recognition. You start seeing familiar configurations faster. A T-Square jumps out immediately. Stellium concentrations become obvious. Aspect webs reveal their structure at a glance. The mechanics become smoother even as the interpretation remains nuanced.

What also develops is humility. The more you know, the more you realize how much impacts location experience beyond what astrology can predict. Economic circumstances, health situations, family obligations, career opportunities, cultural factors, pure chance—all these shape outcomes alongside astrological patterns. Mastery includes acknowledging astrology's limits while trusting its profound insights.

And what definitely develops is intuition based on experience. You've seen enough charts, tracked enough relocations, watched enough transits play out that you develop a sixth sense for what will work. You can't always explain why you recommend waiting six months or choosing the seemingly less obvious location, but your accumulated pattern recognition guides you toward wisdom that transcends the technical analysis.

Using Your Mastery Wisely

With this level of knowledge comes responsibility. You can now see people's vulnerable points—where their charts show wounding, limitation, struggle. You can see where they're set up for difficulty, where timing works against them, where their configurations create inevitable challenges.

Use this knowledge compassionately. Yes, tell people the truth about their challenging aspects and difficult transits. But always connect challenge to growth, restriction to necessary maturation, crisis to breakthrough potential. Nobody benefits from astrological fatalism that says "This will be terrible and there's nothing you can do about it." Everyone benefits from honest guidance that says "This will be demanding, here's what it's trying to develop in you, and here's how to work with it consciously."

Remember that you're consulting real people making real decisions that impact real lives. That job offer in Austin, that relationship possibility in Paris, that escape plan to somewhere entirely new—these aren't abstract astrological puzzles. These are people's hopes, fears, dreams, and desperate attempts to create better lives. Meet them with both expertise and empathy.

And remember that sometimes the most masterful thing you can do is simplify. Not every consultation requires discussing Arabic Lots and special point aspects. Sometimes someone just needs to know their Moon line will feel emotionally nurturing, and that's enough. Mastery includes knowing when less is more, when complexity serves and when it overwhelms.

The Path Forward

You're not done. This book gave you the framework, but mastery develops through application. Every chart you analyze teaches you something new. Every relocation you track adds to your understanding. Every transit activation you witness refines your interpretation.

Keep studying. Not just astrology, but psychology, mythology, human development, cultural studies—everything that deepens your understanding of how people grow and change. The richer your framework for understanding human experience, the more skillfully you'll apply astrological technique.

Keep tracking outcomes. Document your predictions. Note what manifests as expected and what surprises you. The gap between prediction and reality teaches you what you're missing, what you're overemphasizing, what factors you haven't yet learned to weigh properly.

Keep questioning your assumptions. Just when you think you understand how a particular aspect pattern works, you'll encounter someone who experiences it completely differently. Stay curious. Stay humble. Stay willing to revise your understanding based on lived experience rather than clinging to textbook interpretations.

And most importantly, use astrocartography in your own life. Move to your challenging lines when you're ready for growth. Test your easy lines when you need restoration. Track how your transits shift your experience of different locations. You can't truly master this work without living it yourself. Theory only takes you so far. Embodied understanding makes you masterful.

Your Journey Continues

Mastery is not a destination—it's a relationship with the work that deepens over time. You'll have days when you see patterns with crystal clarity and days when everything feels confusing. You'll have consultations where your guidance proves profoundly helpful and consultations where you miss something obvious. This is normal. This is the path.

What matters is that you keep showing up to the work with dedication, curiosity, and willingness to keep learning. What matters is that you use your knowledge in service of helping people make wiser choices about where they live, when they move, and how they work with the opportunities and challenges geography activates in their charts.

THE POWER OF PLACE: MASTER 199

You've done something remarkable by working through this book. Most people studying astrocartography never learn about aspect activation, transit timing, or configuration analysis. They stay at the surface level, reading planetary line meanings from a book without understanding the hidden architecture determining actual experience. You went deeper. You did the hard work of learning to see the invisible patterns that shape geographic experience.

That depth will serve you for the rest of your life—whether you're consulting professionally, helping friends and family, or simply navigating your own location decisions with sophisticated awareness. The gift you've given yourself is seeing the world through astrological eyes that understand how place, time, and soul intersect.

The maps are in your hands. The transits are in motion. Your aspect web remains your constant companion, revealing how each geographic activation will uniquely shape your experience. And now you have the wisdom to read those maps, time those transits, and honor those aspects with consciousness and skill.

Go forth and practice your mastery. The world is vast, your chart is unique, and the intersection of the two holds infinite possibilities for discovery, development, and fulfillment. Trust what you've learned. Trust what you continue to learn. Trust that mastery unfolds not through certainty but through ever-deepening engagement with this profound work.

Your perfect places await. And now you know how to find them.

Glossary

Astrological Terms and Definitions

This glossary provides definitions for key astrological and astrocartography terms used throughout The Power of Place: Navigate. Terms are organized alphabetically for easy reference.

A

Angular Lines: Planetary lines that run along the four angles of the chart—Ascendant (ASC), Descendant (DSC), Midheaven (MC), and Imum Coeli (IC). These are the strongest astrocartography activations.

Annual Profections: An ancient timing technique that moves the angles of your chart forward one sign per year of life, activating different house themes annually.

Apex Planet: In a T-Square configuration, the planet that receives squares from both ends of the opposition. This planet represents the focal point of maximum pressure and growth potential.

Ascendant (ASC): The eastern horizon at the moment of birth. Planetary lines on the Ascendant activate personal identity, physical appearance, and how you initiate experiences.

Aspect: The geometric angle between two planets in a natal chart. Major aspects include conjunctions (0°), sextiles (60°), squares (90°), trines (120°), and oppositions (180°).

Aspect Web: The complete network of aspects connecting a single planet to all other planets it aspects in the natal chart. Understanding your aspect web reveals how planetary line activation affects multiple chart factors simultaneously.

B

Black Moon Lilith: The lunar apogee representing rejected aspects of self, shadow material, and authentic power refusing domestication. Can be calculated as Mean Lilith or True Lilith.

C

Cardinal Signs: Aries, Cancer, Libra, Capricorn. Cardinal energy initiates, acts, and creates change. Cardinal T-Squares create crisis through competing initiatives.

Ceres: The largest asteroid in the main belt, governing nurturing, nourishment, mothering, grief, and the relationship with food and body.

Chiron: The 'wounded healer' asteroid representing core wounds and healing potential. Chiron lines bring wounding to conscious awareness for transformation into teaching and medicine.

Chiron Return: Occurs around age 50 when transiting Chiron returns to its natal position. Represents a critical healing integration period when wounds transform into wisdom.

Conjunction: An aspect where two planets occupy the same degree (0° apart). Represents fusion, intensification, and combined expression of planetary energies.

D

Descendant (DSC): The western horizon, opposite the Ascendant. Planetary lines on the Descendant activate partnership, relationships, and how you relate to others.

E

Earth Signs: Taurus, Virgo, Capricorn. Earth energy builds, manifests, and creates tangible results. Earth stelliums emphasize practical achievement and material success.

Elements: The four basic qualities in astrology—Fire (inspiration, action), Earth (manifestation, stability), Air (intellect, communication), Water (emotion, intuition).

Eros: Asteroid governing passionate desire, creative drive, and the magnetic pull toward what excites you.

F

Fire Signs: Aries, Leo, Sagittarius. Fire energy initiates, creates, and inspires. Fire stelliums emphasize passion, confidence, and spontaneous action.

Fixed Signs: Taurus, Leo, Scorpio, Aquarius. Fixed energy persists, maintains, and resists change. Fixed T-Squares create stubbornness and difficulty releasing patterns.

G

Grand Trine: A configuration of three planets forming an equilateral triangle (120° apart), all in the same element. Creates natural flow, ease, and talent that can manifest as genius or wasted potential depending on consciousness.

H

Harmonious Aspects: Trines (120°) and sextiles (60°) that create flow, ease, and natural cooperation between planetary energies.

House-Based Stellium: Three or more planets clustered in the same house regardless of zodiac signs. Changes with relocation as house positions shift geographically.

I

Imum Coeli (IC): The lowest point of the chart, representing home, family, emotional foundations, and private life. Planetary lines on the IC activate domestic and internal themes.

J

Juno: Asteroid governing committed partnership, marriage, equality in relationships, and power dynamics within partnership.

L

Lot of Eros: Calculated point revealing destiny-level passionate desire and what you're fated to pursue with magnetic intensity.

Lot of Marriage: Calculated point describing where partnership becomes a destiny question and where you encounter significant life partners.

Lot of Spirit: Calculated point representing spiritual purpose, conscious will, and where soul values find expression.

Lunar Nodes: The North Node (evolutionary growth direction) and South Node (comfort zones, familiar patterns). Form an axis representing the soul's karmic journey.

M

Mean Lilith: The averaged position of Black Moon Lilith, smoothing the Moon's elliptical orbit. Most commonly used in astrology software.

Midheaven (MC): The highest point of the chart, representing career, public life, reputation, and life direction. Planetary lines on the MC activate professional themes.

Missing Leg: In a T-Square, the empty point directly opposite the apex planet. Developing the qualities of this sign and house provides relief and resolution for the entire T-Square pattern.

Mixed Aspect Pattern: When a planet has both harmonious and challenging aspects simultaneously, requiring nuanced interpretation and conscious navigation.

Modalities: The three modes of expression in astrology—Cardinal (initiating), Fixed (maintaining), Mutable (adapting).

Mutable Signs: Gemini, Virgo, Sagittarius, Pisces. Mutable energy adapts, changes, and responds flexibly. Mutable T-Squares create scattered energy and difficulty maintaining focus.

N

Natal Aspects: The geometric relationships between planets in your birth chart that remain constant throughout life and fundamentally modify how planetary lines manifest geographically.

Nodal Return: Occurs approximately every 18.6 years when transiting Lunar Nodes return to their natal positions (ages 18-19, 37-38, 56-57, 75-76). Marks profound evolutionary crossroads.

North Node: Represents evolutionary growth direction, areas requiring development, and the soul's intended path forward.

O

Opposition: An aspect where two planets are 180° apart. Creates polarity, tension, and the need to balance competing energies. Weight of 6 points in the aspect weighting system.

Orb: The allowable degrees of separation for an aspect to be considered active. Tighter orbs (0-3°) create stronger, more consistent activation than wider orbs (6-10°).

Outer Planets: Uranus, Neptune, and Pluto. Move slowly, creating generational influences and long-term transformation when transiting natal planets.

P

Pallas Athene: Asteroid governing wisdom, strategy, pattern recognition, and creative intelligence.

Part of Fortune: Calculated point representing natural luck, flow, and where good fortune comes easily.

Personal Planets: Sun, Moon, Mercury, Venus, Mars. Move quickly and represent core personality factors. Weight of 4 points in the aspect weighting system.

Psyche: Asteroid governing soul development, deep psychological integration, and transformation through trials.

R

Relocated Chart: A chart calculated for a different geographic location than your birthplace, showing how planetary positions shift into different houses.

S

Saturn Return: Occurs approximately every 29 years when transiting Saturn returns to its natal position (ages 28-30, 57-60). Marks major maturation and life restructuring periods.

Sextile: An aspect where two planets are 60° apart. Creates opportunity and potential that requires conscious activation. Weight of 2 points in the aspect weighting system.

Sign-Based Stellium: Three or more planets clustered in the same zodiac sign regardless of house positions. Remains consistent across all geographic locations.

Social Planets: Jupiter and Saturn. Bridge personal planets and outer planets, representing growth and structure. Weight of 2 points in the aspect weighting system.

South Node: Represents comfort zones, familiar patterns, and skills mastered in past lives or early development. Can enable stagnation if over-relied upon.

Special Points: Calculated points and asteroids beyond the ten traditional planets, including Lunar Nodes, Chiron, Vertex, Part of Fortune, Black Moon Lilith, Juno, Ceres, Pallas, Vesta, Eros, and Psyche.

Square: An aspect where two planets are 90° apart. Creates friction, tension, and dynamic pressure requiring integration. Weight of 6 points in the aspect weighting system.

Stellium: Three or more planets clustered in the same sign or house, creating concentrated energy and personality intensification in that area.

T

Transit: The current position of a planet in the sky as it moves through the zodiac, creating temporary activations of natal chart patterns.

Trine: An aspect where two planets are 120° apart, in the same element. Creates natural flow, ease, and harmonious cooperation. Weight of 4 points in the aspect weighting system.

True Lilith: The actual, oscillating apogee point of Black Moon Lilith. Less commonly used than Mean Lilith but preferred by some astrologers for precision.

T-Square: A configuration where two planets oppose each other while both square a third planet (the apex). Creates intense pressure, dynamic tension, and powerful growth potential.

V

Vertex: A calculated point representing fated encounters, destiny experiences, and significant meetings with people or situations. The point where fate and free will intersect.

Vesta: Asteroid governing devotion, focus, sacred practice, and commitment to what matters most.

Void-of-Course Moon: When the Moon makes its final aspect in a sign before changing signs. Avoid initiating important relocations during void Moon periods.

W

Water Signs: Cancer, Scorpio, Pisces. Water energy feels, intuits, and connects emotionally. Water stelliums emphasize emotional depth, psychic sensitivity, and spiritual connection.

Weighting System: A systematic methodology for evaluating which aspects dominate when a planet has mixed aspect patterns, using orb tightness, aspect type, planet type, and configuration involvement.

Index

This index provides chapter references for major topics, concepts, and techniques covered in The Power of Place: Navigate. Topics are organized alphabetically with relevant chapter numbers.

A

Air Grand Trines, Ch. 11

Air Signs, Ch. 11, 12

Air Stelliums, Ch. 12

Angular Lines, Ch. 1, 2

Annual Profections, Ch. 7

Apex Planet, Ch. 10

Apex Planet Line (living on), Ch. 10

Arabic Lots, Ch. 7

Ascendant (ASC), Ch. 1, 2, 8

Aspect Orbs, Ch. 2, 6, 9

Aspect Patterns, Mixed, Ch. 6

Aspect Web, Ch. 1, 2, 3

Aspect Web Document (creating), Ch. 2, 15

Aspect Weighting System, Ch. 6

Aspects, Challenging, Ch. 5

Aspects, Harmonious, Ch. 4

Aspects to Special Points, Ch. 9

B

Balancing Strategies (for stelliums), Ch. 12

Black Moon Lilith, Ch. 7, 9

Breakthrough vs. Breakdown, Ch. 10

C

Cardinal Signs, Ch. 10

Cardinal T-Squares, Ch. 10

Case Studies, Ch. 14

Ceres, Ch. 7, 9

Challenging Aspects, Ch. 5

Chiron, Ch. 7, 9, 13

Chiron Return, Ch. 7, 13

Chiron Transits, Ch. 13

Client Consultations, Ch. 10, 11, 12, Conclusion

Complex Lines, Ch. 15

Configurations, Ch. 10, 11, 12

Conjunctions, Ch. 2

D

Decision Matrix, Ch. 8

Decision-Making Process, Ch. 8, 14

Descendant (DSC), Ch. 1, 2, 8, 14

Dominant Aspect Type (determining), Ch. 6

E

Earth Grand Trines, Ch. 11

Earth Signs, Ch. 11, 12

Earth Stelliums, Ch. 12

Elements, Ch. 11, 12

Eros, Ch. 7, 9

Ethical Considerations, Ch. 7, Conclusion

F

Fire Grand Trines, Ch. 11

Fire Signs, Ch. 11, 12

Fire Stelliums, Ch. 12

Five-Step Decision Process, Ch. 8

Fixed Signs, Ch. 10

Fixed T-Squares, Ch. 10

G

Grand Trines, Ch. 11

Grand Trine Activation Principles, Ch. 11

Grand Trine Element Strategies, Ch. 11

Grand Trine Timing, Ch. 11

Growth-Work Lines, Ch. 15

H

Harmonious Aspects, Ch. 4

Healing Work, Ch. 7, 13

House-Based Stelliums, Ch. 12

House Relocation Strategy, Ch. 12

I

Imum Coeli (IC), Ch. 1, 2, 8, 14

Integration Practices, Ch. 6

J

Juno, Ch. 7, 9

Jupiter Transits, Ch. 8, 13, 14

L

Lines to Avoid (when), Ch. 10, 15

Lines to Choose (when), Ch. 10

Lot of Eros, Ch. 7, 9

Lot of Marriage, Ch. 7, 9

Lot of Spirit, Ch. 7, 9

Lunar Nodes, Ch. 7, 9

Lunar Transits, Ch. 8, 13

M

Mars Transits, Ch. 8, 13

Mastery, Conclusion

Mercury Transits, Ch. 8, 13

Midheaven (MC), Ch. 1, 2, 8, 14

Missing Leg (T-Square), Ch. 10

Mixed Aspect Patterns, Ch. 6

Modalities, Ch. 10

Multi-Planet Stelliums, Ch. 12

Multiple Configurations (charts with), Ch. 11

Mutable Signs, Ch. 10

Mutable T-Squares, Ch. 10

N

Natal Aspects (definition), Ch. 1, 2

Natal Chart Analysis, Ch. 2

Neptune Transits, Ch. 13

Nodal Returns, Ch. 7, 9

Nodal Transits, Ch. 13

North Node, Ch. 7, 9

O

Opposition Aspects, Ch. 2, 5

Opposition Planet Lines (T-Square), Ch. 10

Optimal Timing Windows, Ch. 13, 15

Orbs, Ch. 2, 6, 9

P

Pallas Athene, Ch. 7, 9

Part of Fortune, Ch. 7, 9

Personal Timing Calendar (creating), Ch. 15

Planetary Lines (basic understanding), Ch. 1

Pluto Transits, Ch. 13, 14

Professional Assessment Protocol, Ch. 7, 9

Professional Guidance, Ch. 10, 11, 12, Conclusion

Psyche, Ch. 7, 9

R

Recovery Locations, Ch. 14

Relationship Decisions, Ch. 14

Relocated Charts, Ch. 12

Relocation Strategy, Ch. 8, 12, 15

S

Saturn Return, Ch. 13

Saturn Transits, Ch. 8, 13, 14

Sextile Aspects, Ch. 2, 4

Sign-Based Stelliums, Ch. 12

Solar Transits, Ch. 8, 13

South Node, Ch. 7, 9

Special Points, Ch. 7, 9

Square Aspects, Ch. 2, 5

Stelliums, Ch. 12

Stellium Activation, Ch. 12

Stellium by Element, Ch. 12

Stellium Lines (when to choose/avoid), Ch. 12

Stellium Timing, Ch. 14

Strategic Timing Guidelines, Ch. 8, 10, 11, 13

Support Systems, Ch. 10, 13

T

Timing Calendar (creating), Ch. 15

Timing Considerations, Ch. 10, 11, 13

Transit Activation, Ch. 3

Transit Density, Ch. 10

Transit Timeline (creating), Ch. 13

Transit Timing, Ch. 8, 13

Transit-by-Transit Guide, Ch. 8, 13

Trine Aspects, Ch. 2, 4

T-Squares, Ch. 10

T-Square Dynamics (understanding), Ch. 10

T-Square Lines (when to choose/avoid), Ch. 10

T-Square Modality Strategies, Ch. 10

T-Square Timing Considerations, Ch. 10

U

Uranus Transits, Ch. 13

V

Venus Transits, Ch. 8, 13, 14

Vertex, Ch. 7, 9

Vesta, Ch. 7, 9

Void-of-Course Moon, Ch. 13

W

Water Grand Trines, Ch. 11

Water Signs, Ch. 11, 12

Water Stelliums, Ch. 12

Weighting System (aspect), Ch. 6

Worksheets and Action Steps, Ch. 15

www.ingramcontent.com/pod-product-compliance
Lightning Source LLC
Chambersburg PA
CBHW031426150426
43191CB00006B/412